Cambridge Elements ☰

Elements in Ancient Egypt in Context
edited by
Gianluca Miniaci
University of Pisa
Juan Carlos Moreno García
CNRS Paris
Anna Stevens
University of Cambridge and Monash University

T0287023

SCRIBAL CULTURE
IN ANCIENT EGYPT

Niv Allon
The Metropolitan Museum of Art
Hana Navratilova
University of Oxford and University of Reading

CAMBRIDGE
UNIVERSITY PRESS

Shaftesbury Road, Cambridge CB2 8EA, United Kingdom

One Liberty Plaza, 20th Floor, New York, NY 10006, USA

477 Williamstown Road, Port Melbourne, VIC 3207, Australia

314–321, 3rd Floor, Plot 3, Splendor Forum, Jasola District Centre,
New Delhi – 110025, India

103 Penang Road, #05–06/07, Visioncrest Commercial, Singapore 238467

Cambridge University Press is part of Cambridge University Press & Assessment,
a department of the University of Cambridge.

We share the University's mission to contribute to society through the pursuit of
education, learning and research at the highest international levels of excellence.

www.cambridge.org
Information on this title: www.cambridge.org/9781009074537

DOI: 10.1017/9781009070614

First published 2023

A catalogue record for this publication is available from the British Library

ISBN 978-1-009-07453-7 Paperback
ISSN 2516-4813 (online)
ISSN 2516-4805 (print)

Scribal Culture in Ancient Egypt

Elements in Ancient Egypt in Context

DOI: 10.1017/9781009070614
First published online: November 2023

Niv Allon
The Metropolitan Museum of Art

Hana Navratilova
University of Oxford and University of Reading

Author for correspondence: Hana Navratilova,
hana.navratilova@bodleian.ox.ac.uk

Abstract: This Element seeks to characterize the scribal culture in ancient Egypt through its textual acts, which were of prime importance in this culture: writing, list-making, drawing, and copying. Drawing upon texts, material objects, and archeological evidence, this Element will touch upon main themes at the heart of the study of this culture, while building on current discussions in literacy and literary as well as social history.

Keywords: Egypt, culture, literacy, knowledge, writing

ISBNs: 9781009074537 (PB), 9781009070614 (OC)
ISSNs: 2516-4813 (online), 2516-4805 (print)

Contents

Introduction

'Love writing, hate pleasure!' entreats the writer of Papyrus Lansing as he celebrates the scribal profession.[1] Despite our imperfect understanding of ancient Egyptian grammar and limited grasp of its vocabulary, we nevertheless aspire to find traces of the men who wrote, read, copied, and disposed of these texts and the scribal culture they formed.[2] Their traces are evident in their texts, turns of phrase, and handwriting; however, their textual actions – reading, writing, copying, and others – are more elusive than any text or the hand that wrote it. Such textual actions cease to exist as soon as they end. Still, they appear as a significant aspect of ancient Egyptian culture in texts, images, autobiographical inscriptions, and literary compositions. This Element thus takes this prism of textual actions as its starting point and main organizing feature.

In more ways than one, this Element builds on our previous study of the ancient Egyptian scribal culture.[3] In both works, we take inspiration from current trends in literacy studies – specifically, New Literacy Studies – and focus on scribes and writing culture as diverse and ever-changing social phenomena.[4] However, while our previous book examines this diverse culture through ten biographies of ancient Egyptian scribes (real and fictional) and their literacies, this Element looks at this phenomenon through different textual actions. Through this vantage point, writing and the other textual actions with which it is associated appear to cut across different social realms but mostly remain an (inter)personal matter.

To explore these scribal practices, we alternate microhistorical views with explorations of broader patterns within certain textual practices. In Section 1, we lay the groundwork for the main themes of this Element, exploring the polysemy of zh^3, the ancient Egyptian verb for 'writing' and 'drawing'. Through its different meanings, zh^3 comes to light as much more than laying words on a surface, but inherently a socially embedded action in ancient Egypt. In Section 2, we turn to the textual action of writing through a close reading of one text, its phraseology, and the material traces it bears.

Section 3 shifts its gaze to the pervasive practice of enlisting. With extensive archaeological evidence and visual representations, list-making appears as the most significant textual act in ancient Egypt that places its writers within a seemingly document-oriented administration and an intellectual tradition. Since the polysemy of zh^3 points to the close association between writing and

---

[1] *mry zh³.w msdi ³b.w* (Papyrus Lansing = pBM EA 9994, 1, 8); Gardiner 1937: 100; Caminos 1954: 374.
[2] With varying approaches, see Eyre 2013, Pinarello 2015, Dorn and Polis 2016, and Ragazzoli 2019, to name a few.
[3] Allon and Navratilova 2017.
[4] On New Literacy Studies, see discussion in Allon 2019: 7–10.

drawing, Section 4 investigates this visual practice through three case studies in which writing and drawing share a surface.

Section 5 turns again to ancient Egyptian textual production and considers ancient Egypt's manuscript culture, which subsists and transmits through copying. Traditionally condemned as secondary and corruptive, copying has won a place of its own in recent decades, becoming an object of inquiry in studying the circulation of texts and their contexts. The final section, Section 6, considers ancient Egyptian textual engagement through a different viewpoint, focusing on the modern readers of these ancient texts. Reading the scribal culture from an Egyptological perspective raises questions regarding what could be assumed to be shared between the two communities and the complications for Egyptologists that these assumptions invite.

The various views of writing and its subsequent acts recall other words penned by the dancing-averse writer of Papyrus Lansing: 'Therefore, I spend the day telling you: "Write", (but) it seems like a sore (in) your heart. As for writing, it is exceedingly pleasant.'[5]

Writing as a pleasant (or an excruciating) endeavour or an object of one's love is more typical of texts that focus on writing within the context of the scribal profession, such as the so-called *Late Egyptian Miscellanies*.[6] The following sections show a broader appreciation of writing, but we hope some of the pleasant (with some sore-like) aspects of writing are still detectable.

1 Defining

𓏞 *sš (zš)* vb. <u>write</u>, Urk. I, 232, 14 (𓏞𓏞); <u>RB</u> 112, 16; <u>Urk</u>. IV, 252, 3 (𓏞𓏞); <u>inscribe</u>, I, 16,4; 67, 14; <u>paint</u>, 39, 3; Louvre C15, 8; <u>draw</u>, Sin. L2; <u>enrol</u> troops, <u>Urk</u>. IV, 1005, 3; 1006, 3
(Faulkner, *A Concise Dictionary of Middle Egyptian*)

Opening a text with a dictionary definition is almost always a mistake. Overused in high schoolers' and students' essays, quoting dictionaries is deemed lethally dull to the reader.[7] However, even cases of bad writing teach a powerful lesson: writing is rarely just an act of placing words on a piece of paper. The entry just quoted proves this point precisely; the ancient Egyptian verb *zẖ³* (here transliterated as *sš*) includes the acts of writing, inscribing, and enrolling among its meanings.[8] The entry also refers to painting and drawing, suggesting that writing and drawing

---

[5] *ẖ[r] wrš=i (ẖr) ḏd n-k zẖ³.w / sw mj ẖ<s>d jb=k / jr zẖ³.w p³y nḏm.w r-jqr* (pBM EA 9994, 3.10–4.1); see Popko in the *Thesaurus Linguae Aegyptiae* (TLA) 2022.

[6] Ragazzoli 2019.

[7] 'Don't bore your audience to death,' warns Jean Wyrick. 'It's a terrible way to go' (Wyrick 2016: 265).

[8] See Faulkner 1962: 246, whose dictionary is 'sufficiently concise to be reasonably portable and not excessively costly' (vii). The discussions that follow are based on additional sources noted in Wb 3, 475.6–476.15; Meeks 1980–2: 77.3859, 78.3811, 79.2767; Hannig 2003: 1218–19; and the relevant slips and new entries in the TLA.

are the same concept. Their differing translations would reflect the translator's world view, which sees two separate actions, whereas the ancient Egyptian lexicon sees one.

However, the verb's occurrences cluster around specific meanings, each with its conceptualization of *zḫ³* and its products. Alongside the various translations, the entry indicates specific instances of this verb and its relevant meanings. In the first instance (*Urk I*, 232, 14), the king orders a proclamation to be written down, while the last instance (*Urk IV*, 1006, 3) speaks of a military official enrolling troops. In one, it produces a record; in the other, it creates a soldier.

zḫ³, therefore, should be considered polysemic. Any discussion of the verb immediately draws other terms into the mix, such as 'literacy', 'text', 'artist', and 'scribe', each with its history and challenges.[9] To try and alleviate these endless complexities, we will focus on instances of the Old Kingdom (*c.*2649–2130 BC). In this period, we argue, the occurrences of *zḫ³* seem to cluster in three groups.[10] One involves lists, another decrees, and a third monuments. Each of these clusters involves its own set of actors and relationships. Throughout these clusters, *zḫ³* – whether translated as writing or drawing – arises as a socially embedded activity, but in all, context is key.

1.1 Scribes, Kitties, and Palettes

A biographical inscription from the Old Kingdom exemplifies the challenges at the heart of this pursuit. Inscribed on a false door from the tomb of Nekhebu, the inscription describes various tasks with which the king entrusted the official. Among the projects he carried out, he mentions constructing mansions and overseeing the digging of canals.[11] Nekhebu credits his rise to prominence to the years he spent as an apprentice to his brother. Miriam Lichtheim translates his words:

> When I was in the service of my brother, the Overseer of Works . . ., I wrote (*zḫ³*) and I carried his 'palette'. Then, when he was appointed Inspector of Builders, I carried his measuring rod. Then, when he was appointed Overseer of Builders, I was his companion. Then, when he was appointed Royal Architect-Builder, I governed the village for him and did everything in it for him efficiently.[12]

---

[9] Each of these terms also calls for its own extensive bibliography, which extends beyond what this Element could cover. For entry points into these discussions, see Pinarello 2015 and, more recently, Polis 2022.

[10] One could also describe these as nodes, building on Bruno Latour's terminologies within actor-network theory (ANT); see Latour 2005.

[11] See Dunham 1938 and, more recently, Abdelmoniem 2020.   [12] Lichtheim 1988: 13.

The title of his brother, Overseer of Works (*jm.j-r'-k³.t*),[13] has often been translated in the Egyptological literature as 'architect'. Lichtheim and others described Nekhebu as an architect as well based on his engagement in large-scale construction projects, which could have called upon architectural know-how. The text, however, does not clarify whether Nekhebu served his brother in this capacity. As Nigel Strudwick has recently shown, this title more probably spoke to one's command over the large workforce involved in such projects in its organization.[14] Indeed, Nekhebu mentions reckoning his brother's possessions a few sentences down the text as well as governing a town for him. Without a clear definition of what he has written or drawn in the service of his brother, we are at a loss regarding *zh³*'s exact meaning here.

The palette (*š꜀*) and the measuring rod (*m³.t*) seemingly illuminate Nekhebu and his brother's practice. However, their translation depends entirely on our understanding of the title and the verb *zh³*. The word *m³.t* might be an unusual writing of *m³w.t*, 'staff'.[15] Its translation as 'measuring rod' is elsewhere unattested, and it follows Dows Dunham, who notes that staffs 'would be carried by the owner' and not his brother or apprentice, and therefore a different translation would be necessary.[16] Similarly, he reads *š꜀* as 'palette', noting that this instance would be the only occurrence of this word having such a meaning.[17] Our understanding of *zh³* in this passage is circular since it relies on titles and adjacent terms, which, in turn, rely on *zh³* for their translations.

š꜀ was most probably translated in this fashion since palettes are central to images of drawing and writing (see Section 4). In the hieroglyphic script, the palette is employed when writing the verb *zh³* and its derivatives. The hieroglyph (𓏜) represents an archaic form of the scribal outfit, comprising three parts held together with a string: (a) a palette with circular depressions for red and black inks,[18] (b) a holder for reeds, and (c) a bag to hold the ink pebbles.[19] The script seems to prioritize ink as the primary medium for drawing and writing, in contrast to the term *hieroglyph*, whose Greek etymology relates it to carving and engraving, like many texts written in this script were.

---

[13] Jones 2000: no. 944.   [14] Strudwick 1985: 247–50.

[15] Though one should keep in mind that ancient Egyptian orthographies were never standardized.

[16] Dunham 1938: 4, n. 14.

[17] Elsewhere, the scribal instrument is called *mnhd* (Wb 2, 83.3). Here, Sa appears with the [Wood] classifier (Gardiner M3). Following other instances of *š꜀* or *š꜀.t* with a different classifier (Gardiner Y1), it could also be read as a 'document' (Wb 4, 418.10–419.19).

[18] Ink is used here to designate the material employed in the writing process, even though its component and consistency might differ from other forms of ink.

[19] The form is attested as early as the First Dynasty; see Regulski 2010: 213, 717.

The link between $z\underline{h}^3$ and the palette need not be as straightforward as it might seem from their numerous co-occurrences. The nuances of this relationship resonate with questions the philosopher Stanley Cavell raised regarding our ability to comprehend meaning from words repeated in various contexts.[20] He describes an interaction with his eighteen-month-old daughter, who seemingly learned the word 'kitty' after he uttered that word while pointing at the family cat. After a few days of saying and pointing, she seemed to have added a new word to her vocabulary. How to comprehend her understanding of the word 'kitty', he asks, when she later pets a fur piece and exclaims, 'Kitty!'? Did she not understand what 'kitty' means, or did she think 'kitty' means 'fur' or 'soft'? Or perhaps she meant to say, 'the fur piece is LIKE a kitty'. Furthermore, how did the situation appear from her point of view? In many ways, we are like Cavell's daughter in her first attempts at acquiring a language with limited cues; our hopes of reaching proficiency are sadly much slimmer.

We thus struggle to pin down what Nekhebu means when he says 'I $z\underline{h}^3$' not so much because of his lack of precision. Rather, our difficulties are inherent to our lexicographical effort, which is based on collecting the occurrences of a word and deducing meaning from its repetitions. We are therefore confronted with similar problems when trying to understand the verb $z\underline{h}^3$ and its derivate $z\underline{h}^3.w$, 'scribe'. The latter appears, for example, as one's title, self-standing or in a compound tying it to an institution or a role, and seems to mean, literally, 'one who writes'. However, as Stephen Quirke points out, scribes appear at various levels of the administration, and their responsibilities seem to encompass much more than mere writing.[21] Like with many ancient Egyptian titles, as we have seen with the Overseer of Works, we often stumble when attempting to define the tasks and responsibilities entrusted to this role. Massimiliano Pinarello therefore proposed to avoid a single-word translation and refer to scribes as performers of writing activities.[22] Even there, one could ask what part of their role was writing and if writing was entrusted only to them. Therefore, the title 'scribe' raises a myriad of questions on its own, which this short Element will not be able to cover.

Admittedly, our evidence reflects only a fragment of the written evidence, which is, in turn, a thin sliver of the ancient Egyptian cultural production with its oral practices and traditions. To fill in the gaps, we often read these texts with

---

[20] Cavell 1979: 171–3.
[21] Quirke (2004b: 15) has therefore suggested replacing 'scribe' with 'secretary' in order to reflect the broad range of positions held by these title holders between the office secretary and the secretary of state.
[22] Pinarello 2015.

Figure 1 Poultry yard in the tomb of Hezi (Kanawati and Abder-Raziq 1999: pl. 56)

our concepts of texts, art, writing, and drawing. To trace *zẖꜣ*'s contours, one needs to progress slowly – focusing here on one period of Egyptian history – the Old Kingdom – closely observing how meanings are inferred from its occurrences. We will leave out other words of the same root, such as *zẖꜣ.w*, 'scribe', or *zẖꜣ.w*, 'writings', and focus on the act of *zẖꜣ* itself. Similarly, this section will only incorporate images in which the verb *zẖꜣ* appears. Through this laborious analysis, three central meanings arise, which the following sections will explore.

1.2 Counting, Accounting, and List-Making (*zẖꜣ m*)

A scene in the Sixth Dynasty tomb of Hezi depicts *zẖꜣ* near a poultry yard full of geese (Figure 1).[23] Hezi, who served as Judge and Scribe of Royal Documents before becoming Vizier, had his tomb chapel decorated with various scenes relating to offerings and provisions. The scene shows four men sitting in a roofed enclosure with their pens in action, while *zẖꜣ* is noted in their accompanying inscriptions. Though all men engage in a similar activity, the inscriptions call upon a different nuance of writing, highlighting the challenges in interpreting texts and images and their relationship.

Much like in the scene in the tomb of Hezi, *zẖꜣ* appears most often in Old Kingdom art in scenes relating to agriculture and provisions. In the tomb of Ankhmahor, for example, it appears alongside scenes of bread-making, and on the stela of Mery (Louvre B 49b–c), the inscription mentions invocation offerings for various festivals.[24] Other scenes include fowl in Rashepses and Kagemni, weighing grain in Niankhkhnum and Urarna, cattle in Sabu (CG 1419), metal in Mereruka and gold or gold jewellry in Akhethetep (Louvre E 10958), and cloth and bread in Ptahhotep.[25] Finally, similar scenes appear in

---

[23] Kanawati and Abder-Raziq 1999.

[24] Ankhmahor (Kanawati and Hassan 1997: pl. 38); Mery (Ziegler 1990: 114–17).

[25] Rashepses (LD 2, pl. 61a); Kagemni (Harpur and Scremin 2006: fig. 496); Niankhkhnum (Harpur and Scremin 2010: fig. 447; pl. 86); Urarna (Davies 1901: pl. 16); Sabu (CG 1419;

the pyramid complexes of Sahure and Pepi II, where instead of scribes or officials, a goddess, Seshat, enacts the '*zḫ³* of the number of captives who are brought from all foreign lands'.[26] Whether in royal or non-royal art, *zḫ³* is common in scenes that relate to recording and list-making (see Section 3), which is spelled out in a relief from the tomb of Hetepka, showing three men with writing equipment enacting '*zḫ³* of reckoning (*ḥsb*)'.[27]

However, as Kent Weeks notes, ancient Egyptian tomb art never represents all of an activity's parts; instead, key scenes stand for the whole range.[28] This variety of aspects is reflected in the inscriptions in Hezi's scene. One text reads, '*zḫ³* of the poultry which is in the pond', another reads, '*zḫ³* of the poultry for the storehouse',[29] and a third reads, '*zḫ³* of the poultry for the archive (*pr-mḏ³.t*)'. Without the texts, we would not have considered the archive or storehouse relevant to this action of *zḫ³*. We might wonder, then, what other aspects are relevant to *zḫ³* but are not represented in the scene, or which aspects appear in this scene but are not seen as relevant to *zḫ³*. Therefore, while Hezi's tomb seems to offer an evident semblance between *zḫ³* and enlisting, the rules of this language-game – to borrow Ludwig Wittgenstein's terminology – might not be what we assume them to be.[30]

The mention of the archive in Hezi's tomb also shows how textual engagement often extends beyond the very act of *zḫ³*. In Egyptological literature, writing is often associated with notions of permanence and efficacy, especially when hieroglyphs are involved. Here, a less permanent form of writing seems to be involved, one that relies on pen and ink but whose product is to be stored in the archive, at least within the world constructed in the tomb.

Writing is also often emphasized in recent literature as a tool of power and control.[31] Social hierarchy is evident in how the scene from Hezi's tomb represents the men who engage in *zḫ³* differently from those who feed the geese at the poultry farm. The former are better dressed and have full heads of hair, while the latter are shabbier in every respect, suggesting a lower social

---

Borchardt 1937: 100, pl. 21); Mereruka (Kanawati et al. 2010: I. pls. 21 and 74); Akhethetep (Ziegler 1993: 118–19, 121); Ptahhotep (LD II, 103a). Altogether *zḫ³ m* appears in twenty references, two of which are royal (see below). Similar scenes appear in other tombs, but since *zḫ³* does not appear in them, their relevance to this inquiry is limited. Scribes also appear with their title (*zḫ³.w*), but the text describes the scene as *jp*, 'assessing', and *jt̞.t ... r ḥsb*, 'seizing ... for reckoning' (Harpur 1987: 513, fig. 162).

[26] Borchardt 1910: II, pl. 1 (mCairo 39531); Jéquier 1938: pl. 38.   [27] Martin 1979: pl. 11 (9).

[28] Weeks 1979.

[29] Following Grunert, TLA 2022, who reads *wḏ³* as 'storehouse'. Kanawati translates *wḏ³* as 'prosperity', which best fits its accompanying classifier (Gardiner Y1); however, such phraseology is unattested elsewhere.

[30] Succinctly defined as 'language and the activities into which it is woven' (Wittgenstein 1953 [2009]: §7).

[31] See discussions in Bowman and Woolf 1994.

status. However, *zẖꜣ* is often embedded in the scene alongside other activities in a way that does not signal an asymmetrical power relationship. For example, a dialogue in the tomb of Akhmahor shows men engaged in bread-making. One of the bakers in the scene turns his head back to the seated writer and says, '*zẖꜣ* the utterance: I have made six measures of pezen bread.'[32] Here, the bread-maker instructs his colleague to make a record.

Throughout these occurrences, therefore, *zẖꜣ* appears as a socially embedded act. However, as the scene from Hezi's tomb shows, we are often left to wonder how *zẖꜣ* relates to the adjacent image of writing, where they differ, and where they overlap. One of the main obstacles in interpreting these scenes lies in the fact that *zẖꜣ m*, 'registering, list-making', is mainly restricted to tomb scenes. Other contexts bring forward different notions of *zẖꜣ*.

1.3 Royal Command (*zẖꜣ* and *wḏ*)

In Hezi's tomb, *zẖꜣ* mostly involved men writing alongside workmen and artisans. In another context, the verb involves different actors, including the king. A few inscriptions from the end of the Old Kingdom and the beginning of the First Intermediate Period present the intersection of royal power and local politics. Inscribed on the walls of the temple of Min in Coptos, one such decree reads:

> (As for) any official, scribe of the king's document, overseer of scribes of fields, overseer of scribes of everything that is sealed, or functionary, who will receive a levy or who shall write (*zẖꜣ.ty.fy*) orders (*wḏ.w*) to place (*wḏ.t*) the names of the overseer of priests, the inspector of priests, functionaries . . . for any work of the domain of the king – it is conspiring in a rebellious matter.[33]

The ordinance protects the priesthood and more broadly dependants of the temple from any levy work. In its context, *zẖꜣ* is reserved for *wḏ.w* – royal communications ranging from orders to letters of instructions and formal memoranda[34] – where it is associated with the executive power that could put people to work.

Two additional texts make a similar direct connection between *zẖꜣ* and royal power. One text comes from the impressive funerary complex of Sennedjemib's family, who served as vizier under Djedkare Izezi at the end of the Fifth Dynasty. This text is described as a copy of a *wḏ*, which the king

---

[32] Kanawati and Hassan 1997: pl. 38.

[33] JE 43052 (see note on its accession number in Chioffi and Rigamonti 2020); appearing in Goedicke 1967 (87–116) as Koptos B, lines 24–9. A similar text appears in Koptos C (117–19).

[34] Vernus 2013.

issued to him: '[Izezi] made a [*wḏ*] for me, which his majesty himself wrote with his two fingers, in order to praise me for everyth[ing] which I had done [estimably], well, and thoroughly.'[35] The relationship between royal agency and *zḫꜣ* moves here from executive power to signs of a direct and interpersonal relationship between those whom *zḫꜣ* brings together: Senedjemib and the king, who wrote the *wḏ* in his own hand.

A similar notion is evoked in Rawer's tomb, in which an inscription[36] tells of a staff held in the king's hand accidentally touching the official's foot.[37] Immediately, the king exclaimed: 'Be sound!' and ordered that he would not receive so much as a blow for this mishap. Following his speech:

> His Majesty ordered (*wḏ*) it to be put in [writing] (*wd.t m [zḫꜣ.w]*) on his tomb that is in the necropolis. His majesty caused a document (a) there [to be made], written (*zḫꜣ*) beside the king [him]self at the stoneworks of Pharaoh, in order to be written (*zḫꜣ*) in accordance with what [was] said in his tomb in the necropolis.

Even though the king does not write the text, it is drawn up at his request and in his presence. Similarly, many of the Coptos decrees end their texts with the designation 'sealed in the presence of the king himself', pointing once again to the personal involvement of royal power. Rather than abstract royal power, *zḫꜣ* and *wḏ* mark a close and interpersonal relationship between an official and his king.

Rawer's king had, in fact, two texts written. In addition to drawing a document, the king has the text inscribed on Rawer's tomb wall, thus associating *zḫꜣ*, a royal gift, and monumentality.[38]

1.4 Tombs and Other Monuments (*zḫꜣ* and *jz*)

The connection between writing and monumentality is central to current discussions of ancient Egyptian texts and the writing system. Often, this monumental writing is associated with permanence and performativity – the power of the words to enact reality by being written in stone. However, the Old Kingdom discourse surrounding *zḫꜣ* and monumentality conjures other notions that more closely relate to the interpersonal relationship seen in Section 1.3.

A fragmentary inscription in Senedjemib's tomb, for example, reads, according to Ed Brovarski: 'My Majesty has seen this letter of yours

---

[35] Brovarski 2001: I. 90–2.
[36] A detailed analysis of this (in essence royal) inscription located in a dignitary's tomb is provided by Stauder-Porchet 2021a.
[37] Allen 1992.   [38] Note Stauder-Porchet 2021a: 315, 322, 324–7.

which you wrote (*ir.n=k*) in order to inform My Majesty of everything that you have done in drafting the decoration (*qd zḫ³*) of the Hathor chapel of Izezi, which is on the grounds of the palace.'[39] Brovarski translates the term *qd zḫ³* as 'drafting the decoration' while noting that others propose to render it as 'inscription' and 'inscriptional (?) decoration'. Brovarski relates the disagreement in translation to the polysemic nature of *zḫ³*, meaning both 'writing' and 'drawing'. However, the issue here arises from the ambiguity inherent to most instances of *zḫ³* in a monumental context, in which a whole monument is the product of *zḫ³* – in this case, a chapel for Hathor.

Another example of this ambiguous meaning of *zḫ³* comes from the funerary realm. In the tomb of Kahep (Tjeti-Iker) in Hawawish, the object of *zḫ³* is neither a command nor a list but rather a whole tomb:

> The *zḫ³.w-qdw.t* Seni says:
> It is I who *zḫ³* the tomb of the nomarch Kheni.
> It is I, moreover, who *zḫ³* this tomb alone.

Dimitri Laboury discusses this inscription and others like it in his recent studies of artists in ancient Egypt.[40] Like others, he confronts the ambiguity of *zḫ³* but offers a third translation. In his rendering of this passage, Seni *designed* the tomb.

Seni's significance for this discussion also relates to his title, *zḫ³.w-qdw.t*, often rendered as 'draftsman' or 'scribe of forms (or outlines)'.[41] As before, titles call to mind the proverbial broken reed. Here, the title's etymology does not offer much relief since *qd* refers in the Old Kingdom to one's character or nature and not to a drawing's outline or form. More importantly, one assumes here that the nature of Seni's title dictated his activity in the tomb. However, in the tomb of Memi in Akhmim, *zḫ³* is done by the eldest son, whose title is mentioned, and in Tomb H24 in Hawawish, it is a scribe of the divine archives of the palace who carries out the *zḫ³* activity and not a *zḫ³.w-qd* Similarly, Senedjemib carried out the *zḫ³* of a chapel without bearing this title.

A similar claim appears in the tomb of Nebemakhet in Giza, in which two men appear revering the deceased:

> His intimate (friend) who *zḫ³* for him this tomb, the *zḫ³.w-qdw.t* Semerk(a)
> His intimate (friend) who made for him this tomb with works ... Ink(a)ef[42]

---

[39] Brovarski 2001: I. 92.   [40] Laboury 2016 and 2022.   [41] Laboury 2016: 379, n. 22.
[42] Hassan 1943: fig. 78.

Like in our first examples of *zḫꜣ* and list-making, art and text are joined here. However, one would not have assumed that *zḫꜣ* is depicted in the scene without the inscription since the image depicts no textual action.

Whether they meant *zḫꜣ* as 'drawing', 'inscribing', or 'designing', none of these men in this section, *zḫꜣ.w-qd* or kings, present *zḫꜣ* as a performative act, as an action that creates or changes a reality by the very act itself. In contrast, the various men who carry out *zḫꜣ* of a monument do so for their friends, family members, or king, with *zḫꜣ* appearing again strongly as an interpersonal action.

1.5 Filling in the Gaps

In the short story 'Funes the Memorious', Jorge Luis Borges portrays a man who has lost his ability to generalize after falling off his horse. Due to his head injury, his memory became too powerful since he could suddenly remember absolutely everything. 'He was disturbed by the fact that a dog at three-fourteen (seen in profile) should have the same name as the dog at three-fifteen (seen from the front).'[43] The narrator concludes that while there was nothing but details for Funes, 'to think is to forget a difference, to generalize, to abstract'.

In many ways, we might suffer from similar afflictions due to an opposite condition. We find it hard to generalize *because* we are lacking in detail. Our picture lacks the numerous interactions in which *zḫꜣ* took part, not only those written in texts and on monuments but also in spoken interactions. Even the different paths to its meanings suffer from divergent obstacles: text and image compositions play a significant role in one context and are entirely denied in another, specific terms are significant in some contexts, and ambiguous terms bring a variety of translations in others.

Throughout its three clusters of meaning – list-making, order-writing, and monumentality – the social realm arises as the central aspect. It binds working men within a scene, a king and his official, or men decorating or inscribing a tomb for their friends and family. The social context is very much what mostly escapes us as we try to think back to what *zḫꜣ* meant in ancient Egypt.

Returning to the beginning of this section, we should ask whether *zḫꜣ*'s polysemy is inherent to the Egyptian term or inflicted by the modern reader. This section has shown, we believe, that different clusters arise already in the ancient texts. Such meanings might appear in the same context (Senedjemib and Rawer), but the action of *zḫꜣ* in them is different enough in their object and the actors they pull together.

---

[43] Borges 1962 (1956): 36–8.

Once again, Wittgenstein's models of meaning might be of help here. Instead of meanings being clearly differentiated and defined, we might think of the relationship between *zḥꜣ* and its situated meanings as family resemblance. One family member might resemble others, for example, in hair colour and not in height, and another in their eyes but not their mouth. Similarly, the various meanings of *zḥꜣ* overlap but remain somewhat apart.

The following sections will continue to chart out the different actions *zḥꜣ* has come to take in ancient Egypt in the Old Kingdom and beyond this period: writing, copying, drawing, and others. There – as here – similarities and overlaps abound, but the paths to our understanding of them are never straightforward.

2 Writing

'In writing one must create an endlessly changing surface.'

(Power, *Conversations with James Joyce*)

James Joyce's call for dangerous writing could not seem more foreign to ancient Egypt. In his conversation with Arthur Power, the famous novelist calls modern authors to take every risk.[44] One must abandon classical modes of writing and create an endlessly changing surface, he says, in order to express the flux to which everything is inclined nowadays. Also, an Egyptian writer, Khakheperreseneb, wishes for new forms of speech that would give voice to one's present experience.[45] 'Would that I had unknown utterances, extraordinary sayings, and new language that does not pass away, free from repetition, without a saying of transitory speech that was spoken by the ancestors.'[46] He does not want to repeat the words that have already been used, even if they have a distinguished cultural pedigree. His heart is also ambiguous about the value of the past and its writers: 'Antiquity passes, yet weighs heavily.'

However, the failure of the classics is a sign of the troubled world in which he lives and not of literature itself. For Joyce, the endlessly changing surface is the author's goal; for Khakheperreseneb, it is the reflection of his misery, and yet, despite their differences, the two share a similar view of texts and forms as fixed in their meaning.

The very notion of fixed meanings has long been contested by various twentieth-century writers like Jacques Derrida and Umberto Eco.[47] Because of the open-endedness inherent to texts, myriad practices often surround them to

---

[44] Power 2001 (1974): 90.

[45] Translation in Parkinson 1997; 144–50; Parkinson 1996c; compare Hagen 2019b.

[46] Hagen 2019b: 194.   [47] See, for example, Derrida 1978; Eco 1989.

(a)

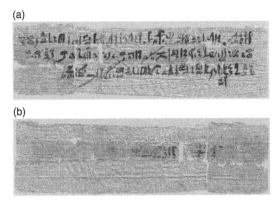

(b)

Figure 2 Front and back sides of Tit's letter to Djehuti; New Kingdom,
Eighteenth Dynasty, joint reign of Hatshepsut and Thutmose III
(*c*.1479–1458 BC). From Deir el-Bahri, temple of Hatshepsut, in rubbish near
foundation deposit 9, MMA excavations, 1926–7, Roger's Fund 1927
(MMA 27.3.560)

ground their interpretations. Consider the codified interpretations of the Bible or
certain Egyptological readings of ancient Egyptian literary texts, to name a few.

Textual open-endedness is not a fixture of literary texts only. An ancient Egyptian
letter of the Eighteenth Dynasty (MMA 27.3.560) offers a view into this matter
from the vantage point of the writer, who needs to raise a delicate issue:[48]

> [1] Tit informs his Lord Djehuty l-p-h through the favor of Amun-Re; This
> letter is to cause that [2] my Lord knows the matter concerning Ptahsokary; to
> the extent that: It is indeed you who transgressed him among the people of [3]
> Heliopolis;[49] Speak with the Herald Geregmennefer, so that you (two) send
> a letter about it to the Greatest of Seers (High Priest of Heliopolis).

The letter speaks of a bureaucratic storm that ensued after a man named
Ptahsokary was wronged, engulfing at least four other men: Tit, the letter's
writer; Geregmennefer, who is to compose another letter on this matter; the
Heliopolitan high priest, who is not named; and Djehuty, the letter's addressee
and possible culprit.

Writing feels especially dangerous when Tit appears to place blame on this
higher-ranking official and possibly one of the sovereign's prominent men in
a flurry of construction projects.[50] Such a message can be easily misunderstood

---

[48] For translation, commentary, and bibliography, see Hafemann 2023.
[49] For alternative readings of this sentence, see more below.
[50] The addressee here is assumed to be Djehuty, the Overseer of the Treasury and Overseer of
Works who was involved in Hatshepsut's building campaigns (Shirley 2010: 195) and the owner
of Theban Tomb 11 (Galán and Díaz-Iglesias Llanos 2020).

or read as an affront to a superior. To anchor his message, Tit seems to have left various markers in his choice of words and corrections, the text's materiality, and the ink's flow.[51]

This section will follow these markers in the writing process from the moment before the pen is put to 'paper' until it is put down and the document readied to serve its purpose. Through its various stages, writing appears to be more than drawing signs on a papyrus; it is a negotiation of one's own standing through the medium of an endlessly changing surface.

2.1 Before

Before even writing the first sign, Teti had already started fashioning his message to Djehuty. Such inceptive moments are thematized in a few literary texts.[52] In the *Prophecy of Neferti*, the king wishes to write Neferti's description of what will happen. To do so:

> He stretched out his hand to a box of writing equipment. Then he took a **scroll** and a **palette**. He then put into writing what the lector priest Neferti said.[53]

Similar materials are readied in another instance when the king instructs the high official Rensi to delay judgment so that he could bring a record of the Eloquent Peasant's speech for him to enjoy. At the end of the text, Rensi presents the peasant's truly perfect words written on a new papyrus roll.[54]

Texts in ancient Egypt were not limited to papyri, and similar letters were found on ostraca – broken sherds and chippings of stone – which were more readily available alternatives. The material, therefore, did not dictate the genre as papyri often contained accounts, medical and magical texts, and religious and literary compositions, as Neferti and the text of the Eloquent Peasant both describe and are written on. However, papyri seem to be quite an incidental expenditure for the elite, better suited for carrying a written message elsewhere.[55]

Tit picked a papyrus roll of a size that fits the nature of his text.[56] Eighteenth Dynasty Papyri could measure around 36 centimetres in height,[57] but they were often quartered or halved for easier handling, as is the case here. The height of Tit's letter only measures 4.5 centimetres, but its breadth of 17.5 centimetres suggests he began writing his letter by turning the papyrus sideways, as did many of his contemporaries. The papyrus could then unroll from his lap

[51] Olsen (2018) suggests the context here is that of workmen arriving from other sites in Egypt to take part in the ruler's building projects in Thebes.
[52] For a discussion of framing devices in ancient Egyptian texts, see Hagen 2013.
[53] Goedicke 1977. For a recent discussion of an Eighteenth Dynasty copy of a text, its materiality, and further bibliography, see Hassan 2017.
[54] Parkinson 2012 (B2, l. 128–30).   [55] Compare Haring 2015.   [56] Krutzsch 2016.
[57] Parkinson and Quirke 1995: 16.

forward.[58] This choice is reflected in Tit's papyrus, whose letter runs perpendicularly to the upper fibres.

With the papyrus laid out before him, Tit was ready to write, but a final decision needed to be made. Nowadays, ancient Egypt is known for its hieroglyphs, thanks to their iconic nature and use on monuments. In ancient times, this elaborate script was more restricted in its usage, and hieratic – the cursive script of ancient Egypt for most of its history – was far more common. In fact, literate men who wrote hieratic possibly faltered if they needed to write hieroglyphs, and it has been suggested that most people began their education in hieratic. Tit made the (only) reasonable choice of writing his letter in the cursive script.

2.2 In Process

This brief communication does not reveal the events that led to its writing. Was a group of Heliopolitan temple workmen sent to Thebes by the Greatest of Seers, as William Hayes suggested?[59] Was Ptahsokary their leader? How did Djehuty offend him if, indeed, he is to blame? The problem required the involvement of a few high-ranking officials, including Djehuty, and Tit chose to perform his lesser status through a common turn of phrase: (Tit) *ḥr swḏꜣ jb n nb=f*, '(Tit) greets his lord.' Tit did not fail to mention the favor of Amun-Re, one of the primary gods of Egypt's New Kingdom, to whom many temples were dedicated in Thebes, where this letter was found.[60] Even though these phrases might have long lost their literal meaning – much like the more recent 'I hope this note finds you well' – they still set a proper tone that was very appropriate.

Alongside his choice of words, Tit was attentive to the mechanics of writing. As he began writing his letter to Djehuty, he dipped his pen and first put his name on the papyrus.[61] Even before he penned all seven signs that write out his name, his ink started running low. He chose to redip his pen, as is evident in the contrast between the faint curved hieratic sign in the first line and the following thicker dot – the hieratic classifier of male personal names (Moeller 33, corresponding to Gardiner A1 in hieroglyphs, 𓀀).[62]

Such contrasts appear regularly throughout the first line, suggesting Tit redipped his pen three more times before reaching the end of this line of the text. The sign of a beaky bird on a standard (𓅜) stands out, for example, in the first line, and a progressively fading *ḥsw.t* (𓎛𓇓𓏏) is followed by a thick reed leaf writing the name Amun (𓇋𓏠𓈖). Compare, however, how the contrasts in

---

[58] Bakir 1970: 19–22.   [59] Hayes 1957: 90.

[60] According to Bakir (1970: 55), other letters often would add *m* before ꜥ-w-s.

[61] Or perhaps it was even half a dip, since shortly after he redipped his pen again.

[62] For classifiers, see Goldwasser 2002, and, more recently, Goldwasser and Grinevald 2012; Lincke and Kammerzell 2012.

the second line between thicker and fading signs are visible but much less stark. While a rhythm governs the first line, the rest of the letter and the second line especially seem to indicate much more frequent redipping.

This close attention to thick and fading signs does not only bear witness to the materiality of writing. It may also indicate Tit's involvement in his own text and hint, in some instances, at oral and written predecessors of a manuscript. In one of the groundbreaking close studies of writing and its materiality, James Allen analyses the letters of Heqanakht, whose eight complete documents and five fragments shed unparalleled light on the lives of a wealthy estate owner in Middle Kingdom Egypt.[63] In his close study of the signs, Allen notes:

> In firsthand documents there is a more immediate relationship between the author's thoughts and their written transcription. Because of this immediacy, autographed manuscripts may display a somewhat different pattern of brush usage and emendations. The flow of the ink can be comparable to that of dictated manuscripts when the author's thoughts themselves flow smoothly, but it may be more irregular when the scribe is 'thinking on paper', less certain of what to say.[64]

Allen contrasts autographed letters with dictated ones, which show a more regular flow of ink with fewer stops to 'think on paper'. It seems reasonable to assume Tit wrote his own letter, but discerning whether the letter was dictated or autographed is admittedly subjective; one might wonder, for example, whether dictations might not invite moments of hesitation for the one dictating or the one writing it. Nevertheless, Tit's letter seems to suggest that his attention to the letter's wording regained focus following the introductory sentences.

Tit's concentration in the second line might relate to more than just the difficulties of composition. In another critical study of writing practices, Chloé Ragazzoli offers a complementary view of writers and their work: '[W]hen one is involved in the meaning of what one writes, the tendency will be to stop at meaningful places, with the risk of a less regular ink density or some fading of this density'.[65] In Ragazzoli's account, the ink flow is more than a side effect of the writing process. Writers respond to this material aspect but could also choose to redip in meaningful places and highlight vital matters in the text. For example, new sentences in our text seem to begin with instances of redipping:

[(1)] **Tit** informs his Lord **Djehuti** l-p-h through the favor of **Amun-Re**
   This letter is to cause that [(2)] **my** Lord knows the matter concerning Ptahsokary;

---

[63] Allen 2002.   [64] Allen 2002: 81.   [65] Ragazzoli 2017a: 106.

To the extent that it is indeed you who transgressed him among the people
of [(3)] Heliopolis;

Speak with the Herald Geregmennefer,
so that you (two) send a letter about it to the Greatest of Seers[66]

As Tit dipped and redipped his pen to write this brief missive, he was also
attentive to the words themselves. None of them continue into the following
line, and when he came to write the word 'Heliopolis' towards the end of
the second line where the remaining space was limited, he wrote it – without
redipping – at the beginning of the third line.

Tit was also attentive to the signs, especially the classifiers he placed at the
end of words. Like in other hieratic texts of the Eighteenth Dynasty, most words
appear in this letter with at least one classifier. *jmn* 'Amun', for example, is
followed by a divine classifier (Moeller 188, Gardiner G7 ⟑) on the first line; *rḫ*,
'to know' is classified by the rolled papyrus sign (Moeller 538, Gardiner Y1 ⟷)
on the second, and *jwn.w*, ''Heliopolis' with its city sign (Moeller 339, Gardiner
O49 ⊛) on the third.[67]

In a few instances, Tit curiously employs different hieratic signs that seem
otherwise entirely interchangeable.[68] For example, the classifier for *ḥsw.t*,
'praise, favor' on the first line and ▨▨ *mdw.t*, 'words, matter' on the second
resembles its hieroglyphic counterpart showing a man with his hand to his
mouth (Moller 35, Gardiner A2 🖼). In contrast, a more abbreviated writing of
this sign appears three times on the third line after ▨▨ *mdw*, 'speak', *wḥm*,
'Herald', and the particle *kꜣ* ▨▨.[69] It is hard to discern whether these differences
are motivated – for example, *ḥsw.t* and *mdw.t* are nouns of a similar kind and
ending – or whether these belong to the variations one comes to expect in
ancient Egyptian handwriting.[70]

A more significant variation seems to appear with personal names and the
seated man classifier (Moeller 33, Gardiner A1). The text shows two variants of
this sign: a simplified dot, as, for example, with ▨▨ and ▨▨, Tit and Djehuty's
names, while ▨▨ and ▨▨, Ptahsokary and Geregmennefer's names, receive
a more fully formed classifier, as well as the title of the Greatest of Seers at the
end of the third line ▨▨. This fuller writing of the sign appears in two other
places on this papyrus – in the names of the letter's sender (▨▨) and addressee
that are written on the back but were first to be visible to the reader when

---

[66] This is merely an approximation of the redipping practices in the text. Not only does the word
order differ between English and Egyptian, but this rendering emphasizes estimated moments of
redipping based on clear contrasts in thickness.

[67] *jmn* (Wb 1, 84.15–85); *rḫ* (Wb 2, 442.7–445.7); *jwn.w* (Wb 1, 54).

[68] I am grateful to Daniel González León for sharing his work on signs and their variants in the
hieroglyphic script.

[69] Fischer-Elfert 2021: 336.   [70] Janssen 1987.

receiving the letter. With this distribution in mind, it seems that Tit reserved the fuller writing to the first instance of each name.

As thoughtful and careful as Tit seems to have been so far, his writing was not devoid of errors and emendations. The word *jb*, 'heart'[71] is followed by an unexpected sign of a seated man (), as if the sentence reads, '(Tit) makes greets *myself, his lord'. Similarly, if indeed the letter was to follow the regular formula, the preposition *m* would have been expected before the blessings of l(ife), p(rosperity), h(ealth). A darker shadow around the word *mȝ.w*, 'Seers' at the end of the third line suggests he started writing a word there that he needed to correct and erase.

So far, the main story focused on the hieratic signs and the ink with which they were written. However, another story could be told by looking at the spaces between them. In Tit's handwriting, ligatures are rare, but the signs are regularly placed with limited space between them. Only in two instances might one identify two gaps that are wider than usual on the second line. Admittedly, the additional spaces appear in both cases after the elongated sign writing the third-person pronoun (=*f*). However, no spaces are used in the other two other occasions in which it is employed in this letter (lines 1 and 3). It also seems as if the pen was redipped in this section more than once, and the sentence appears to be the most volatile part of this text: 'It is you who transgressed against him.'

It is even possible – though difficult to prove – that Tit chooses an ambiguous way to convey this message here. Hayes and others following him read the sentence as placing direct blame on Djehuty and his actions. In this case, Tit employs a form of the second-person pronoun (*twt*) that appears in earlier sources rather than the more common pronoun (*ntk*) of his time.[72] It is then possible that he employs this specialized pronoun to perform the hierarchical difference between him and the recipient again while signalling his erudition. Joachim Quack offers an alternative reading to the text that places the accusation against Ptahsokary, 'to whom transgression fits among the men of Heliopolis'.[73] As we ourselves struggle to anchor our own reading of the text, it is hard to discern which reading Tit intended. However, one cannot exclude the possibility that this ambiguity was deliberate. Could it be that Tit purposefully wrote a message that could be understood in two different ways?

2.3 After

As Tit was finishing his letter, it is possible that he had another final look at the text and, to his detriment, noticed a few problems. Perhaps still distracted by the

---

[71] Wb 1, 59.10–60.11.   [72] Stauder 2013a.
[73] Quack, according to Stauder 2013b: 166–7, n. 381; *twt* r jmdm 'gleich' (DZA 30.981.410).

challenging statement, he omitted the proposition 'with' and wrote *wḥm*, 'again' instead of *wḥm.w*, 'Herald'. Perhaps at this point he squeezed in a narrow *w* between the final signs of *wḥm*, but the preposition required more space ▨. He, therefore, added it below the line, accidentally smearing a small quantity of the ink of the two signs above.

Finally, the main text was ready, but writing had not ended yet for Tit. He cut the text from the papyrus roll and folded the letter twice along horizontal lines and then into thirds along vertical lines. While larger papyri were often rolled, letters, documents, and magical texts were folded.[74] With magical texts, it has often been argued that such folding could prevent anything interfering with the magic inside while containing it within the papyrus.[75] Though one would not associate letters with similar concerns of magical efficacy, the folding of Tit's letter similarly maintained the text within its covered surface and thereby anchored it as a direct missive between Tit and Djehuty.

At this stage, Tit added his own name on one side of the folded letter, flipped it, and wrote Djehuty's name on the other. At the final step of projecting and performing his status towards Djehuty, he wrote 'to his lord', marking yet again the hierarchal relationship he had weaved through his text many times before. Moreover, he wrote the pronoun 'his' upwards instead of its otherwise descending line elsewhere (▨). In this final touch, he marked not only his lesser status, but also his relationship to Djehuty, with the line itself leading towards the recipient's line.

Who delivered the letter and how we do not know. When folded, it is as thin as a finger and easy to carry. It was found among mixed materials during the Metropolitan Museum's excavations in Deir el-Bahri near one of the temple of Hatshepsut's foundation deposits. The archaeological context aids in anchoring the text's dating and a possible context for the working relationship between Tit, Djehuty, Ptahsokary, and Geregmennefer.

2.4 Concluding Remarks

If we follow Joyce's vision of an endlessly changing surface, we are another link in the chain of readers of Tit's text, creating new meanings to this brief missive.[76] Without knowledge of the exact circumstance of this letter and the events that led to it, it is impossible to reconstruct how Tit saw the task ahead of him. Through his choice of words, the rhythm of the ink, and the spaces between the signs, we tried to tell a story – among many other possible – of a careful

---

[74] Krutzsch 2008.   [75] Krutzsch 2014.

[76] As was recently emphasized in Margaret Geoga's paper at the seventy-fourth annual conference of the American Research Center in Egypt (ARCE) in Minneapolis, on a panel on the reception of ancient Egypt.

Figure 3 The letter, folded as found (M8 C 331, Egyptian Art Archives,
The Metropolitan Museum of Art)

Figure 4 Dipinti in the North Chapel of Senwosret III, Dahshur east wall
offering list; drawing by Sara Chen and Hana Navratilova
© The Metropolitan Museum of Art

writer who is not devoid of mistakes but is nevertheless attentive to his own
writing. In our vision of Tit's letter, writing exists in its physical manifestation
as well as in the social realm it constructs and performs.

3 (En)listing

The north chapel of Senwosret III's pyramid in Dahshur (*c*.1837–1819 BC)
disappeared in antiquity, serving as a quarry for the Ramesside stoneworkers.
Before being engulfed by the overwhelming need for limestone, it had attracted
visitors through the centuries, many of whom put their names on the reliefs.
Their writing often overlayed the monumental hieroglyphic texts with cursive
signatures, juxtaposing two registers of writing, hieroglyphs and hieratic. At the
same time, it inscribed them into the ancient cult.

A group of such visitors selected an offering list high on a wall with considerable
effort. It was a sequence of provisions for the deceased, organized in a geometric
grid, with accompanying figures of offering bearers. They evidently considered this

list an essential feature; otherwise, their writing would not be directed at it. Moreover, their writings clustered around meat provisions, suggesting they read these lists carefully. However, why were these lists created in the first place? What else, apart from securing eternal sustenance, can a written list stand for in ancient Egyptian culture?

Egyptian lists also attracted the eye of modern scholarship. In Umberto Eco's list of lists, Egypt was represented by an offering list of Princess Nefertiabet,[77] a list with both a visual and a textual aspect, like the list in the chapel of Senwosret III. Nefertiabet and Senwosret remind us that lists appear in both written and visual cultures. Jack Goody's study on early literacy used Egyptian lists, mainly *onomastica*, to claim that writing enabled inventorying on an unprecedented scale and in an unprecedented variety.[78]

The list thus fascinates by its universal, transcultural presence. 'At their most simple, lists are frameworks that hold separate and disparate items together.'[79] There is no end of material things or abstract concepts that we can put in a sort of list; a telephone directory, a dictionary, a shopping list, or a presentation of royal offerings are all lists.[80] Organizing items is a mnemonic tool that can install a sense of comprehensive knowledge and control.[81] As cognitive tools, lists are certainly not a prerogative of the written culture.[82] It is possible to memorize unwritten lists, but the list – certainly for Claude Lévi-Strauss and Goody – becomes particularly powerful in writing. For Michel Foucault, 'a written text is a systematic conversion of the power relationship between controller and controlled into written words'.[83]

Through these discussions, two functions of written lists become clear: as tools of restriction and coercive power and as tools of cognitive development. Emma Brunner-Traut, for example, suggested that the list-loving Egyptians built their culture on a taxative view of the world that had to be described in lists.[84] At the same time, Egyptologists also take lists to represent an underlying catalogued knowledge of the world,[85] time and history (through king lists), and space (a list of *nomes* or foreign subjugated countries).[86] By considering these approaches to written lists, this section will focus on the act of enlisting itself as an activity that creates lists as written artifacts.[87]

---

[77] Eco 2009, from the slab stela no. G 1225 from Giza; Manuelian 2003: 58–63.
[78] Goody 1977: 109.   [79] Belknap 2004: 2.   [80] Eco 2009; compare also Doležalová 2009.
[81] Goody and Watt 1963.
[82] Details in Cohen and Lefebvre 2005. Mnemonics, techniques helping with retention and retrieval of information, developed from simple to more sophisticated from antiquity to the early modern period (Carruthers 2008; Yates 2014).
[83] As summarized by Ezzamel 2012: 12–13.   [84] Brunner-Traut 1990.
[85] Gardiner 1947: 41–6.   [86] Loprieno 2001: 142–4.   [87] Eyre 2013: 350–1.

3.1 Inventorying and Listing

In tomb art, writing men are often represented making lists,[88] while officials were routinely shown presenting them.[89] The accompanying inscriptions clarify that the tomb owner is *m33 zḥ3.w*, 'seeing/inspecting the written record',[90] while they are *rdi.t zḥ3.w*, 'presenting the document' and 'proffering', and *šdi*, 'reciting' them.[91] Within the world constructed on the tomb chapel's walls, list-making is featured as a practice that is crucial to making provisions possible and controllable.[92] The Old Kingdom inspection of documents suggests that the lists, written or visual, had the power to connect and unify the many things that could be listed in all areas of daily existence.

Wooden models of the Middle Kingdom present an interesting case to consider the role of lists and other activities surrounding them.[93] Writing never appears as a separate activity in these three-dimensional images, but it is included in scenes of farming, agriculture, granaries, and ritual. On Meketre's – a Middle Kingdom official buried with many high-quality models – model sailboat, a man presents an unrolled papyrus to a statue of the deceased. Upon closer inspection, the text on the papyrus is a list of offerings (see Figure 5), reading: 'a thousand (pieces) of bread, beer, cattle, and fowl'.[94] The contents – another offering list – situate this scene in the context of a funerary cult; this is a veneration, not an office scene.

Within this represented world, list-making is closely associated with mobility. Physical spaces for administrative activities and specifically for the production and storage of writing are amply attested textually and visually.[95] Yet Jacques Vandier – in his monumental study of Egyptian art – hesitated to assign a 'bureau' as an epicentre of scribal activity,[96] assuming that the Egyptians would not have set registering apart from other daily activities. Indeed, in most scenes, scribes are only surrounded by a bagful of papyri or tablets and the scribal kit. Consequently, list-making scribes were ever-present, emanating from the bureaux to make inventories, thereby inserting themselves into the land's daily life.[97]

While lists and list-making were significant throughout Egyptian history, New Kingdom tomb art stands out for its scope of lists. If, in the Old Kingdom, list-making was predominantly in the service of the tomb owner

---

[88] In other contexts, one can encounter the writing figure of the goddess Seshat in the pyramid complex of the Old Kingdom; see Section 1.

[89] Kessler 1990; Manuelian 1996.   [90] Kessler 1990: 22–3; compare Manuelian 1996.

[91] See the overview in Manuelian 1996: 582–5. The verb Sdj is translated both ways and appears also in the 'Appeal to the Living'.

[92] Compare Kessler 1990: 42–3, who only highlights provisions as the significant aspect of these images.

[93] Eschenbrenner-Diemer 2017: 133.

[94] Compare Manuelian 1996: 571, the model MMA 20.3.4, and Winlock 1955: 60, pls. 45. 49, 50.

[95] Compare Ragazzoli 2019: 135–40 and Eyre 2013: chapter 7.1.   [96] Vandier 1964: 195.

[97] Compare Eyre 2013: 253–7.

Figure 5 List presented in Meketre's model sailboat (detail), Middle Kingdom, Twelfth Dynasty, early reign of Amenemhat I (*c.*1981–1975 BC). From southern Asasif, tomb of Meketre (TT 280, MMA 1101), MMA excavations, 1920, Roger's Fund and Edward S. Harkness Gift 1920 (MMA 20.3.4)

and his estate, New Kingdom officials write lists about the functioning of the state and its military power. Thus, in addition to scribes registering harvests in various Theban tombs, scribes of recruits and prisoners in the tomb appear in the tomb of Rekhmire in Thebes (TT100), in the Saqqara tomb of Horemheb, and in a battle relief on the temple walls of Mediant Habu (Ramesses III).[98] In addition, select dignitaries weave their literacy into their narratives, often through a scene that shows registration.[99] In the context of the proposed double capacity of the list, practical and symbolic, the utilitarian act of inventorying was provided with a monumental representation.

3.2 Lists As Artefacts

Despite the significance of list-making in the visual record, Christopher Eyre questions whether lists and accounts were as vital for Egyptian society and administration as the images on the tomb walls led us to believe. Eyre rightfully notes how rarely texts refer back to documents in archives throughout Egyptian history.[100] Nevertheless, the visual representation of scribes attending so many areas of daily life is mirrored by the material production of documents. From

---

[98] Martin 1989: detail pls. 87–8. For comparable Theban material, see also Hartwig 2004: 76–7.
[99] Hartwig 2004: 78–9.   [100] Eyre 2013.

workmen lists in temple and tomb constructions to catalogs of books in temple libraries, a considerable body of detailed documents that register, list, and account for has survived.[101]

These accounts were not only utilized around the moment of their inception, but many were archived for future use. The archives accompanied temples, palaces, offices, and workshops.[102] The Old Kingdom royal funerary precincts contained extensive archives with papyri bearing lists of deliveries, personnel, people entitled to a share in the temple's offering supply, and equipment lists.[103] They were usually written on papyrus in a careful system of tables, alternating black and red ink, and operating like a sophisticated spreadsheet.[104]

The much-discussed New Kingdom documents from Deir el-Medina represent another wealth of lists centred chiefly on personnel (and thus the organization of work) and supplies (and thus sustenance of the workforce). Writing occurred on papyri, ostraca, and writing tablets, where each medium might have represented a different phase of the writing process.[105] Lists were copied (see also Section 5) between different writing materials, as illustrated in the Deir el-Medina examples: the lists of workmen present and absent at work were noted on ostraca and compiled later on papyri.[106]

3.3 Lists As an Intellectual Concept

The seemingly drab tasks of listing, checking, and putting things in order were not only an indispensable part of the scribal activity, but also a part of ancient Egypt's intellectual formation. Papyri also bore a great variety of lists, especially from the Middle Kingdom onward. The *onomastica* are massive, quasi-encyclopedic lists of words arranged in thematic sequences. Alan Gardiner included the following textual artifacts in his analysis of the *onomastica*:

Ramesseum Onomasticon, P. Berlin 10495	Middle Kingdom	List of animals, fortresses and towns, food, body parts, etc.

---

[101] Papyrus Berlin 9874, Deicher 2015: 11–12. See, for example, Hassan 2016b and Deicher 2015. Compare Ezzamel 1997 and 2012, the latter book notes listing as part of accounting and therefore organizing the lived world.

[102] Hagen and Soliman 2018.   [103] Posener-Krieger 1991; Posener-Krieger et al. 2006.

[104] Vymazalová 2015: 242 f. See also Ezzamel 2012: chapter 9.

[105] See the brief summary of types of writing material in Donker van Heel and Haring 2003: 38.

[106] First suggested by Jaroslav Černý then analysed in detail in Donker van Heel and Haring 2003: 1–5.

Onomasticon of Amenemope on two longer manuscripts. Golenischeff and Hood – BM 10202, both papyri	Late New Kingdom; copies either end of Ramesside or Third Intermediate Periods	(Hierarchical encyclopedia of the world): Sky, water, earth; Persons (court, offices, occupations); Classes, tribes, types of human beings; Egyptian towns, buildings, their parts, and types of land; Agricultural land, cereals, and their products; Beverages; Parts of an ox and kinds of meat
Onomasticon Amenemope, shorter excerpts: BM 10379, leather; Ramesseum papyrus fragments; oCairo J 67100, a potsherd; BM 21635, wooden writing board; P. Boulaq IV	Third intermediate period	See above.

They list the contents of the world and human society and are attested from the Middle Kingdom to the Late Period with differing arrangements.[107] Amenemope's *onomasticon* also provides an insight into the production and materiality of the *onomastica* copies. It has survived on several papyri, albeit fragmentary, a leather roll, an ostraca, and a writing board.[108] The papyrus might have come from a personal library. However, the range of artifacts suggests a wider circulation, including a temple library, where the leather roll might have been consulted more often.[109] Ostraca and writing boards might allude to its part in advanced training, though so-called school texts are more challenging to identify than one would wish.

Whether these specific copies were used for training or not, 'categorization' and list-making can be considered 'intimately tied to learning'.[110] The enlisting present in *Onomastica* and other texts could be read then as closely related to the 'phenomenon of systemization and reorganization that we can find in the

---

[107] Quirke 2004a, 42; *LÄ* IV, 572; Grandet 2018: 127 f.   [108] Gardiner 1947: I. 26.
[109] Compare Eyre 2013: 31–2, 263–4.   [110] Harnad 2005: 22. See also Quack 2015.

Ramesside period and continuing in its most advanced stage in the Third Intermediate Period'[111] and visible also in the system of classifiers.[112]

The *onomastica* also give an idea about the conceptual thought behind enlisting, as they aim 'for the instruction of the ignorant, and for learning all things that exist: what Ptah created, what Thoth copied down'.[113] The verb Gardiner translated as 'copy' is *sphr* (see also Section 5), which appears frequently in the context of lists and, in a particular subgroup of historical lists, the annals (on which see below). Amun may make annalistic record *sphr* for Hatshepsut[114], just as Thoth may *sphr* the created world in the act of making things happen by writing, 'suggesting the idea of a full equivalence between the written word and a physical existence'.[115]

Onomastica could therefore be more readily comparable to early science than philology.[116] *Onomastica per se* are *sbȝy.t*, 'teachings' which call into mind such instruction texts, as the Wisdom of Ptahhotep that served *m sbȝ ḥmw r rḫ, r tp-ḥsb*[117] *n mdt nfrt*, 'in teaching the ignorant to be wise, according to the rules of fine words'.[118] Yet listing and inventorying in Egypt is remarkable for its productivity and role as an epistemic effort.[119] This intellectual effort might also be reflected in other kinds of lists: geographical lists, king lists, and annals. With these significant categories in mind, inventorying and enlisting appear as widespread practices that bleed into religious and magical texts.[120]

I Geographical Lists

The Egyptians had a practical working knowledge of their country's and other regions' geography and displayed it in their visual and written culture. However, they did so in formats fitting their cultural patterns and communication. The overarching representation of Egypt was that of a list of regions protected by deities,[121] hence the subgenre of cultic geographical lists.

The first millennium is rich in texts preserved as temple decoration and on papyri, confirming a well-developed 'canon' of cultic geography.[122] Geographical papyri, such as the Tanis Geographical Papyrus (British Museum ESA 10673), record nomes, their landscapes, and their gods. The Tanis example is fascinating, having been found with 'Tanis Sign Papyrus' (British Museum ESA 10672), suggesting the

---

[111] Chantrain and Biase-Dyson 2017: 51.   [112] Chantrain 2014.   [113] Gardiner 1947: I. 2*.

[114] Redford 1986: 76; see Urk.IV 276:11–12.   [115] Ragazzoli 2019: 248.

[116] It is to be discussed further if or when it did or did not became classificatory, pace Eyre 2013: 51. Cancik-Kirschbaum and Kahl 2018 have examples of early philological work; see Section 5.

[117] On this expression as 'rules for social action' see also Baines 2023 with previous references.

[118] Quirke's translation in 2004a; see also Parkinson 1996b: 301.   [119] Ragazzoli 2019: 265.

[120] Massart 1959; Ragazzoli 2019: 240.   [121] Quack 2008 and 2020.

[122] Leitz 2014; Quack 2020.

existence of a Late Period/Greco-Roman library that contained both these comprehensive lists.[123]

II Genres of Egyptian Historiography

Egyptians' relationship with the past was comprehensive and well articulated.[124] In our current history writing, lists may serve solely as the backbone to understand a historical narrative.[125] Historical writing in ancient Egypt can be said to be interspersed with lists but also as represented *by* lists, to some of which considerable attention to historical detail could be attributed.[126]

Two of its genres – king lists and annals, '*gnwt*' – were, in essence, inventories. A king list is a series of royal names, mainly in chronological order. In the annals, the deeds of kings fulfilling their royal role in Maat were listed in an annual template.

It may be plausibly argued that the use of writing constituted or at least expanded some of the uses of the past.[127] The Royal Canon of Turin, usually considered the only surviving example of an 'archival' king list, does not thematize local cult or cultural memory but provides a historical backbone.[128] Interestingly, it is written on a verso of a papyrus with another list. A taxation list organized most probably in geographical sections is on its recto.

Cultic lists of gods and kings adorned temples and tombs. Some such king lists were adapted for a purpose – for example, the temple or tomb lists referring to locally or dynastically important kings of the past.[129] These lists are perhaps similar to the continually readjusted traditional genealogies.[130] In the same way, geography and history intersected in localized king lists, probably reflecting local religious use (for example, local cult or feasts).[131] Finally, not only kings could be listed for purposes of cultural and connective memory: illustrious ancestors could be listed too.[132]

Another element in Egyptian history writing, the annals, '*gnwt*,' consists of lists of a different calibre. The annalistic record is subject to variations, but it is always a list.[133] The Palermo Stone is akin to stacking dolls. It is a list of kings, each of whom commands a list of regnal years, and each year contains a list of important events. A similar principle of lists nesting within lists is applied

---

[123] Griffith and Petrie 1889. New publication expected by Jasnow and Ryholt – compare British Museum website: www.britishmuseum.org/collection/object/Y_EA10673-3. See also the examples from the Carlsberg papyri collection, Ryholt et al. 2020.

[124] Baines 2011; Popko 2014. Compare Baines 2011b: 587–8, quote p. 589.   [125] Baines 1983.

[126] Redford 1986: xv.   [127] Contardi 2016.   [128] See also Popko 2014.   [129] Redford 1986.

[130] Goody and Watt 1963: 309.

[131] Compare Redford 1986: 45–58, Malek 2000, and Quack 2008.

[132] Fragment Daressy, Redford 1986: 26, PM III^2:571 f.

[133] See Redford 1986: 65–96, Baines 2011a, and Popko 2014.

across other examples of the genre. The annals of Amenemhet II list royal donations and foreign tribute,[134] and the annals of Thutmose III list years of campaigning, campaigns within years, and the military successes within each campaign, plus the tribute income and donations to Amun. Eventually, annals could have been written for the kings, but also – usually by Thoth – for the gods, for example, Osiris.[135]

Other royal inscriptions, especially more complex eulogies, have their role in Egyptian historiography, listing the royal successes; in this case, a list of royal deeds is conducted either over a period of time or in service of a particular deity. The gods may also provide a list for the king, outlining the expectations for what constitutes an effective, successful reign, such as in Amun's injunction to Hatshepsut in the Red Chapel.[136] The kings, in turn, defended their status and ability in a never-ending viva voce examination by the gods and posterity.

The Great Harris Papyrus has a specific standing among list-like documents of Egyptian historiography (and political thought). It is a massive (originally over 40 metres long) written portrait of the reign of Ramesses III. A significant part of this textual compendium, where the king explains his deeds for the gods and his people, consists of enclosures with lists that make evident the royal care for divine cults (exemplified by but not limited to donations) as well as for humanity.[137] The list constitutes proof and confirmation in this royal (auto) biography.[138]

From royal annals to the Great Harris Papyrus, these texts essentially thematize the royal self, but the list was also an essential tool for non-royal self-thematization. Although biographies were not for everyone,[139] those who opted for one of the variants of this genre often deployed a list-like text as part of their rhetorical devices.[140] Whether it was a sequence of epithets, laudatory phrases, an itemized outline of their actions in the service of the king, or fulfilling a righteous life,[141] listing was part of the biographical practice. The practice of lists as building blocks of life-writing is by no means limited to Egypt, but it is illustrated very well in Egyptian examples.

3.4 To Conclude

Eyre has suggested that 'Listing stands as a primary use of writing. In Egypt, listing then provides the core genre for writing knowledge, both

---

[134] Altenmüller 2015.

[135] For example, see Assmann 1999a: 491; Theban tomb 257 (5), PM I: 342.

[136] Lacau and Chevrier 1977: 124 ff.; Redford 1986: 263.   [137] Grandet 1994: I. 44–6, 60–4.

[138] Grandet 1994: 52; Ragazzoli 2019: 240.   [139] Frood 2007.   [140] Gnirs 1996.

[141] On the subject of biographies, see Gnirs 1996, Frood 2007, and Stauder-Porchet, Frood, and Stauder 2020.

administrative and cultural.'[142] As the various lists show, listing was of importance not only practically, but also epistemologically and ultimately ontologically. The acts of registering, cataloging, or listing were performed in diverse settings by many different people. They were all linked by their access to literacy and by their socially sanctioned but individually performed authority.

The applicability of inventorying covered administration and communication with the divine: an understanding of taxation and devotion could be encapsulated in a list. Already early on, the two functions of the list co-occurred. The ritual or offering list seems to appear together with the written record, and geographical lists of sorts (domains) already adorn Old Kingdom royal temples. Yet the proliferation of other lists from the Middle Kingdom and then again from the New Kingdom onwards suggest that the conceptual, epistemic role of the list was gradually amplified.[143]

Egyptian lists also allow for imagining space and time and representing what matters. A catalogue of kings or an inventory of provinces and their gods provides temporal and spatial knowledge. A temple library is more than a mnemo-technical assistant; it is a summary of riches. A list of geographical names captures the knowledge of topography and a geopolitical message.[144] The *onomastica* suggested interest in the organization of the world and of organizing knowledge about the world. Its social hierarchy was recorded in *onomastica*, but it could also be articulated in instruction texts which emphasized the role of the 'scribe'. The instructions of Khety offer the paragon example: 'In the Teaching of Khety, the teacher describes a sequence of wretched workers (4a–21 g); this sorry vision of society has an "answer" in the profession of scribe (21i), but the chaotic illiterate workers are also ordered into a literate, onomasticon-like presentation which is itself a response.'[145]

The text of Khety was copied for millennia.[146] When the literate visitors to the chapel of Senwosret III appended their names to the offering list, they were not looking at a mundane collection of words on the wall. They created a role for themselves in the eternal sustenance of the king. But they also entered a visually organized, governable, meaningful place that symbolized their culture's legacy. Unlike Amenemope in P. Anastasi I,[147] they understood the signs and read the list with a reflection on its meaning.

---

[142] Eyre 2013: 350.   [143] Compare Ragazzoli 2019: 248–9.   [144] Grimal 2006.
[145] Parkinson 1996a: 154.   [146] See a late copy published by Quack 2020a.
[147] Fischer-Elfert 1986.

Ancient Egypt in Context

Figure 6 Column 1 of Papyrus Sallier III (detail); New Kingdom, Nineteenth Dynasty (*c*.1070–1186 BC); purchased from Francois Sallier, 1839 (pBM EA 10181). © The Trustees of the British Museum

4 Drawing

Three horses run awkwardly atop a papyrus (Figure 6). Their bodies are drawn in outline, while thicker pen strokes indicate their ears, muzzles, and manes. Below them, two additional horses appear in the hieratic narrative of Ramesses II's Battle of Kadesh.[148] Only slightly smaller in scale, they are drawn in a similar fashion but as classifiers for the word *ḥtr*, 'horse'.[149] The horses below are signs of writing embedded in the text, but are the three other horses almost identical in form and the product of writing? Or should they all be considered drawings?[150] Given the pictographic tendencies of the ancient Egyptian writing system, distinguishing *writing* from *drawing* in cases like this appears moot.[151]

Writing, however, is multifarious, as this Element argues through its various sections. Letters occupy different contexts than lists. Hieroglyphs often decorate monumental walls, but Egypt's more common scripts – hieratic and demotic – appear on walls in secondary inscriptions, which later visitors added.[152] Similarly, as Sallier's horses show, drawing can refer to a variety of compositions, from signs and figures to scenes, which can hardly be 'read' as texts. *Writing* and *drawing* may pertain to distinct semiotic, social, and material worlds, and their intersections are as varied as they are individually.

These intersections especially come to the fore in ostraca. On monumental walls, the various scripts perform different functions, and on papyri, drawings are mostly restricted to funerary contexts. Ostraca, on the other hand, show a wide variety of both drawing and writing in its various scripts. No single section can do justice to the subject of drawing or its relationship to writing, and

---

[148] Copying a text that is otherwise inscribed on the walls of Abu-Simbel, Karnak, and other temples (see Copying), see Spalinger 2002.

[149] Wb 3, 199.11–200.12.

[150] They could also serve as 'trial' signs and 'doodles,' both of which also exist on the spectrum between writing and drawing.

[151] In other instances, writing and drawing are well distinguished through size, arrangement, and other parameters. See, most recently, Laboury 2022a and 2022b.

[152] See papers in Ragazzoli et al. 2018.

this section will focus on three ostraca from the New Kingdom to explore the relationship and distinctions between *writing* and *drawing* through the ways in which they interact and coalesce. Together, they lead to broader considerations of *writing* and *drawing* whose shared implements, surfaces, and titles indicate the close and complex relationships they play in one's professional as well as social worlds.

4.1 Writing, Drawing, Scribes, and Artists

Discussions of *writing* and *drawing* often swiftly move to focus on those who made them: artists and scribes. At first, it is an easy task to distinguish one from the other through the objects they produce, the materials they employ, and the titles they carry. Scribes (*zḫꜣ.w*) hold red and black ink palettes to write texts, while draftsmen (*zḫꜣ.w-qdw.t*) employ palettes with a wider range of pigments to draw and paint.[153] *Writing* and *drawing* thereby become tied to discussions of titles and objects, which present their own challenges, as noted in Section 1.

Artists' palettes are a case in point.[154] Most wooden palettes from ancient Egypt have two wells for red and black inks and are described as scribal palettes.[155] Much rarer are wooden palettes with larger inkwells, some of which still preserve the remains of various pigments which artists would use.[156]

Both scribal and artists' palettes are represented in scenes on tomb walls, but images of artists' palettes are few and far between. The Overseer of Draftsmen (*ḥr.y zḫꜣ.w qdw.t*), Djehutimes, represents himself twice in his Memphite tomb holding such palettes, once with nine recesses for pigments, the other time with many more.[157] These differ from the image of Iouty in Huya's tomb in el-Amarna, who holds a palette that possibly had only four recesses.[158] Only the latter, in fact, shows such a palette employed in artistic production. More commonly, images of artistic production either show the general shape of a palette with no distinctive features (such as, for example, in the tomb of Neferrenpet (TT 178)) or, more commonly, the so-called scribal palette.[159] Such, for example, are the palettes held by two draftsmen applying pens to the surface of a stand and the back of a statue in a Twenty-Sixth Dynasty tomb.[160] A palette of six oval recesses of the New Kingdom (UC16054) adds to the confusion since its owner, Huy, served as an administrator and not an artist. In addition, palette Petrie UC 16055 shows beautifully drawn hieroglyphs

---

[153] See, for example, Louvre N 3014 (Andreu 2013: 145, no. 17a).

[154] See the discussion on Kha's tomb (TT 78) in Pinarello (2015: 40–2), who notes that Kha's tomb contained two wooden palettes, each with six recesses.

[155] See, for example, MMA 16.10.298, BM EA 5513, and others (see Glanville 1932).

[156] See, for example, BM EA 5512.   [157] Zivie 2013: 34; pl. 54, 57, 73.

[158] Davies 1905: pl. 18.   [159] Hofmann 1995.   [160] See Andreau 2013: 16, fig. 2.

and figures but only has black and red inkwells.[161] These palettes seem, therefore, to move across assumed professional boundaries.

Artists' signatures provide another example of the difficulties at hand. Much like the ancient Egyptian textual production, the visual corpus in ancient Egyptian is more often than not left unsigned without being ascribed to a named person. More recently, Laboury has noted that artists' signatures are more numerous than they might seem.[162] Among these, he includes later visitors' inscriptions of artists who 'signed' their names as they visited monuments, but more importantly, those in which the artist claims to be the one who made the tomb's decoration.

Following the discussion in Section 1, such statements are less conclusive than one would have hoped. Consider, for example, the case of the draftsman Amenhotep, son of Amunnakhte. He left a hieratic inscription on the walls of a Theban tomb of an official named Imiseba, saying he has 'executed (*iri*) the decoration (*zḫꜣ.w*) in the tomb', and whose hand is indeed identifiable in some of the figures and hieroglyphs in this tomb.[163] However, even in this case, Amenhotep does not clearly indicate which part of the tomb he sees as *zḫꜣ.w*.

Moreover, as Tamas Bács indicates, such a graffito is a rarity, and in other cases, such claims do not involve a claim to direct execution of *zḫꜣw*. Paheri, for example, takes pride in caring for the resting place of his illustrious grandfather, Ahmose, son of Ibana.[164] His image appears in Ahmose's tomb holding a palette (with two recesses), and an inscription above says: 'It is his daughter's son who directed works in this tomb while enlivening the name of his mother's father, the draftsman of Amun, Paheri, true of voice.' Here the core of this artist's signature lies in Paheri's title. He is indeed a draftsman, but unlike Amenhotep's claim in Imiseba's tomb, Paheri does not credit himself with the tomb's decoration but instead with directing the works in the tomb. These might include decorating the tomb, but the signature does not emphasize his art. It is, therefore, as if we are reading his inscription backward, assuming that his title dictates his contribution to his grandfather's tomb. Similarly, Seni and his brother, Izezi, speak of how they *zḫꜣ* tombs, but the nature of this verb is not easily evident (see Section 1).

Finally, *zḫꜣ.w-qdw.t* were clearly involved in artistic pursuits, as evident from visual and textual evidence. However, the exact nature of this title and how it was perceived are rarely thematized.[165] A few men carrying such titles left, for example, autobiographical texts, but these are very often focused on the person's social and moral character and their relationship to the king, leaving their

---

[161] Pinarello 2015: 71.   [162] Laboury 2012: 201.   [163] Bács 2011.
[164] Allon and Navratilova 2017: 13–24.   [165] Most recently, Stauder 2018.

Figure 7 Photograph of scene from the tomb of Neferrenpet (TT 178); New Kingdom, Nineteenth Dynasty (*c.*1279–1213 BC); TT 178 (T2878, Egyptian Art Archives, The Metropolitan Museum of Art)

professional activities as artists beyond the scope of the text. The unique text in that sense in Irtisen's stela speaks to images he can make but highlights how little we know.[166]

In most other instances, the title appears alongside characters, like the two men in the aforementioned Twenty-Sixth dynasty tomb, one decorating a stand and the other a statue. Clearly, their actions involve art and pen-and-palette, but how to understand what they are doing? Are they painting the piece – as some have suggested – or perhaps drawing hieroglyphs? A similar question can be raised regarding the man's actions in the scene in Neferrenpet's tomb.

Therefore, while pertinent to our studies of art, artists, and society in ancient Egypt, discussions of palettes and signatures point to the limits of our understanding. They also point to the porous boundaries between artist and scribe and, therefore, between writing and drawing.[167] As Laboury notes, artists in ancient Egypt could also be placed on a broad spectrum of literacies, with some of them speaking of their direct engagement with texts.[168] Within the same vein, but moving away from actors to actions, the following sections explore through ostraca three moments in which writing and drawing come to share one surface.

4.2 Drawing Hieroglyphs (MMA 23.3.4)

Numerous textual and figural ostraca were found in the so-called Hatshesput Hole, mixed in with various discarded materials.[169] Alongside broken statues and disposed-of scarabs and donation pieces, these ostraca were used to level the ground for Thutmose III's causeway in Deir el-Bahri. Some of these ostraca

---

[166] See Stauder 2018 for recent bibliography.
[167] Compare Callender 2019: xii–xiv, who uses 'scribe' and 'artist' interchangeably in her work on hieroglyphic palaeography.
[168] Laboury forthcoming.   [169] Patch 2005.

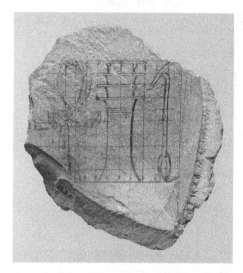

Figure 8 Ostracon with hieroglyphs on grid; New Kingdom, Eighteenth Dynasty, joint reign of Hatshepsut and Thutmose III (*c.*1479–1458 BC). From Deir el-Bahri, so-called Hatshepsut Hole, MMA excavations, 1922–3, Roger's Fund 1923 (MMA 23.3.4)

bear a colourful painting of a hippopotamus (MMA 23.3.6) or a swallow (MMA 23.3.7), while others speak to the work at the site, including lists mentioning the vizier Rekhmire, one of the most prominent figures of this time.[170] Many ostraca are either figural or textual, but one ostracon combines both. The ostracon depicts a sceptre, a pillar, and an ankh strap (or tie) in red and black on top of a grid.[171]

The signs could be read from left to right as hieroglyphs that write the words *ꜥnḫ, ḏd, wꜣs*, 'life, stability, dominion'. Below, a curved line possibly indicates another sign, a basket writing *nb*, 'all', but this sign is neither set within a grid nor marked in black ink, like the others.

Such signs, as Herbert Winlock points out in his discussion of this ostracon's find, are a common appearance on the walls of Hatshepsut's temple in Deir el-Bahri:

> [T]he most instructive of all was a flake on which was worked up a commonly recurring phrase in the inscriptions. The sculptor has tried three signs, altering them to his liking, and then squared them off for transference on to the temple walls, where they can be found today in their finished state.[172]

---

[170] On Rekhmire, see Davies 1943.   [171] Roehrig 2005: 44 (no. 22).
[172] Winlock 1923: 37, fig. 32.

Winlock takes the signs to be written first, followed by the grid. Laying a grid on top of an image is elsewhere attested.[173] However, on our ostracon, the black ink is laid on top of the red grid, not vice versa.

More interestingly, he identifies different steps in this ostracon's production. The ankh sign, for example, is written twice: once in red and another time in black. Red preparatory lines are also evident at the bottom of the middle sign, where the pillar curves towards the ground line. Only the third sign, the *w3s* sceptre, does not seem to have had an earlier draft drawn before it was marked in black. Hayes reads these steps as traces of the artist's process, in which he alters his own signs to his liking. In contrast, Catharine Roehrig suggests the ostracon may have been used to teach 'a young scribe the proper proportions of the hieroglyphs'.[174]

Their differences show a common thread in the interpretation of ostraca and the challenge in interpreting hieroglyphs, especially the ones before us. Very often, red and black markings on a textual ostracon are interpreted as signs of two hands: a teacher and his student, a master scribe and his apprentice, and so forth. Many textual ostraca are indeed read very often as textual exercises and school texts, whereas figural ostraca are more often described as sketches and preparatory drawings. It is, therefore, significant to see that Roehrig locates the ostracon within the textual realm as signs that are written by a student **scribe**, while Winlock contextualizes it within the artistic realm, with a **sculptor** as its producer, testing his own design.

Whether artist or scribe, their remodelling of the ankh sign and preparatory drawings underneath the Djed pillar emphasize the aesthetic nature of this pursuit. The redrawn ankh changes the placement of its horizontal line and width, not its legibility. In fact, one may wonder whether the signs are to be read at all. Each of these icons commonly appears in reliefs, amulets, and other objects, suggesting they might be understood as symbolizing life, stability, and dominion or embodying the concept rather than being read as a text.

4.3 Drawing and Hieroglyphs (MMA 14.6.213)

The ankh, the Djed pillar, and the *w3s* sceptre appear again on another ostracon in the hands of Ptah, whose figure holds the center of this piece from the Valley of the Kings. Here, hieroglyphs appear alongside the deity's figure in a column to the right and the row below. The signs below are written in smaller script but bear yet again the so-called artist's signature of Amenhotep, son of Amennakht, whose hieratic inscription in the tomb of Imiseba was discussed earlier. As this

---

[173] Kanawati and Woods 2009: 34–6, 76.   [174] Roehrig 2005: 45.

(a)   (b)

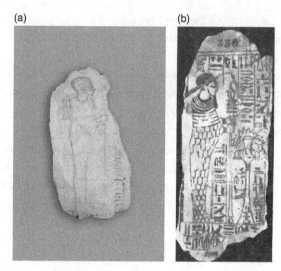

Figure 9 Figured ostraca with an image of Ptah-Sokar; New Kingdom,
Dynasty 19–20 (*c.*1295–1070 BC). From Valley of the Kings. Left, gift of
Theodore M. Davis, 1914 (MMA 14.6.213). Right, CG 25052
(Bruyère 1929–30: figure 31). © IFAO

ostracon might represent a preparatory drawing for another ostracon, it brings to
the fore the wide range of aesthetics in drawing hieroglyphics.

The ostracon depicts the shrouded image of the god Ptah 'in his good name as
Sokar{t}y'. His image is drawn twice, with the red line outlining a figure
rescaled from the waist up. The hieroglyphs to the right are drawn schematically, with the Man with His Hand to the Mouth person sign (Gardiner A2)
reduced to single lines marking the man's body, limbs, and head. The signs
below are partly missing, but the inscription clearly names the Draughtsman
Amenhotep, son of the Scribe of the T[wo] lands [Amennakht].

As Cathleen Keller points out, this ostracon resembles another one from the
Valley of the Kings (CG 25052), also naming Amenhotep.[175] On the Cairo
Ostracon, the god is drawn in much richer detail, and the hieroglyphs are
more fully written. The inscription is longer, but the god's good name appears
in the second column, while the attribution to Amenhotep is mentioned in the
top line below the god's feet. The two ostraca may represent unrelated efforts,
but as Keller suggests, the shared provenance, artist's name, and similar composition suggest our ostracon represents a sketch, a provisional version, of the
Cairo drawing.

---

[175] Keller 1997: 144.

In comparing the two ostraca, writing and drawing seem to point at different aesthetic horizons. Ptah's image in the Cairo Ostracon is beautifully drawn with a feather-patterned cloth and broad collars, the latter only schematically marked in the Metropolitan image. The outline, nevertheless, is very similar in shape and style. In contrast, the fuller hieroglyphs in the Cairo Ostracon do not resemble the ones in the Metropolitan Ostracon, in which most hieroglyphs are made in line drawings or are rather crudely drawn. Interestingly, the word *rn*, 'name', which appears without a classifier in the Cairo Ostracon, is accompanied by the Man with His Hand to the Mouth person sign (Gardiner A2), as it often does in hieratic. In addition, neither of them compares to the volume and detail that appear in the previous ostracon from the Hatshepsut Hole. Only the ankh, the Djed pillar, and the *wꜣs* sceptre that the god holds are similar in style. If, in the previous ostracon, writing and drawing merge, here they are clearly drawn by the same hand, which treats them, nevertheless, with a different level of attention.

Amenhotep's name on both ostraca points at various practices in which drawing and writing share a surface. Figural ostraca were often considered practice sketches or preparatory drawings for a composition before it was painted or carved on a more permanent surface, such as a tomb wall or a stela. In contrast, Keller and others have proposed to see such ostraca as the Cairo piece (and perhaps also the Metropolitan Ostracon) as donation pieces or stele-ostraca.[176] In these instances, the ostraca speak to the dedicator's relationship with the god. By placing his piece in a location of significance, he possibly intends to enhance its efficacy – following Keller's terminology.

As an artist's signature, Amenhotep's name seems to point to the different effects of *drawing* and *writing*. In their context as donation pieces, however, both drawing and writing share similar aims of speaking to Amenhotep's relationship with a god.

4.4 Drawing and Hieratic (MMA 26.7.1453)

The third ostracon combines script and image as well, but the inscription is written entirely in hieratic. The cursive script stands in stark contrast to the royal image that is drawn in great detail with the king's flesh and crown filled with red ink. Therefore, the ostracon speaks to the possible effects of writing hieratic alongside a drawing and the artists' literacies.

The ostracon, which comes from debris near the entrance to Tutankhamun's tomb in the Valley of the Kings, depicts a king spearing a lion. Without laying any grid lines or preparing a preliminary drawing, the skilled artist confidently

---

[176] Most recently, see Bács 2021.

(a)   (b)

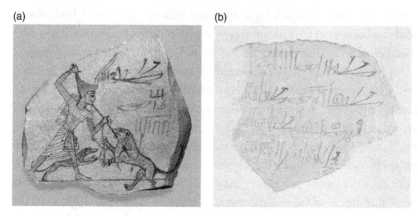

Figure 10 Ostracon with image of pharaoh spearing a lion and royal hymn on its back; New Kingdom, Twentieth Dynasty (c.1186–1070 BC). From Valley of the Kings, debris near the entrance to the tomb of Tutankhamun (KV 62), Carnarvon/Carter excavations, 1920 (MMA 26.7.1453)

drew the king's body in movement as it pushes a spear through the lion's throat. The king's garments are marked in detail, as well as his dog's features and collar. Even the lion's mane and fur are carefully done, with arrows descending into and outside the body they penetrate.

Many ostraca correspond to the decoration of royal tombs in the Valley of the Kings (see 14.6.212). This scene, however, belongs to a different repertoire that is mainly known from royal paraphernalia (Tutankhamun's chest) and minor arts (see, for example, Budapest 2007.1-E with Sheshonq III's name).[177] Like Tutankhamun's chest with its scenes of hunts and battles on opposite sides, the ostracon associates hunting with military success. In the latter, the two are portrayed in imagery side by side, while here, the labour is divided between text and image: the scene shows the hunt while the hieratic inscription reads: 'the slaughterer of all foreign lands, Pharaoh, l-p-h'. The four lines on the back continue to praise the king, comparing him to the sun of every land:

> (My) good Lord l-p-h, the sun of all lands, the ruler l-p-h of that which the Aten encircles, the sunlight is rising, and he brightens the land.

This formulation of royal imagery seems unique to this text, which along with the image, highlights the personal choices of the artist who made this ostracon. Nevertheless, it reflects how well acquainted the writer is with the solar imagery of kingship in this period.[178] Such imagery would not be restricted to the written

---

[177] Cairo JE 61467.   [178] On royal eulogies, see Spalinger 2003.

word, and it is hard to imagine it did not circulate in oral speeches, ceremonies, and royal appearances, but the writer here does not diverge from the phraseology that is familiar in the written royal hymn of this period.

As Laboury argues (see Section 1), one finds artists who can probably read a few hieratic signs and scribes who can produce drawings – like the Sallier horses – with some skill. Here, we are confronted with a man whose literacy encompasses hieratic and possibly hieroglyphic texts while showing great artistic skill. While we can easily distinguish here *writing* from *drawing*, we cannot easily describe him as merely an artist or a scribe. Such a close relationship between professions is even harder to distinguish in the community to which he most probably belonged – the workmen of Deir el-Medina who decorated the tombs of the kings and queens of the New Kingdom.[179]

Therefore, this ostracon reflects the choices of an artist-writer who is well versed in both image and text and their various registers. Though intentions are always hard to pin down, his choice to contrast an elaborate image with a cursive script may reflect a particular attitude towards the text: not as a monumental object, but as a missive of a personal nature.[180]

4.5 Concluding Remarks

As Ben Haring has pointed out, we often tend to diverge our discussions of figural ostraca from those of written ostraca, assuming that literacy and artistic skill are complementary at best.[181] As these ostraca here have shown, their makers approach both writing and drawing in various ways. From drawing hieroglyphs to painting a royal image, drawing also appears to cover a wide range of activities even on one kind of material: stone ostraca from close geographical proximities. Intentions are never clearly laid out, but the first might be a preparatory drawing for carving, while the second – a sketch for another ostracon – might be a dedicatory mini-stela. The third could possibly be also a donation piece, though one that clearly expresses its maker's relationship to the king.

The script shows great flexibility in its ability to move between text and image through the three different pieces. The three signs at the beginning are a case in point: the ankh, djed, and was, which could be read as 'life, dominion, stability', are held by Ptah's hand in the second. The hieroglyphs next to them become so schematic that they almost resemble the hieratic in which the final piece is written. There, the shape of the ankh is so cursive that one probably needs to be a skilled scribe or writer-artist to recognize it.

---

[179] The literature on this site is extensive. For recent research and further bibliography, see Töpfer, Del Vesco, and Poole 2022.

[180] See Allon 2021.   [181] Compare Haring 2020.

Compared with the horses atop the papyrus, there is no question that the ostraca show much greater artistic talent. Nevertheless, the galloping horses remind us that many hands can achieve drawing and that often our interpretation would be affected by the object on which they appear, its context, and their placement on it rather than skill.

5 Copying

So far, our sections have focused on writing and drawing through the objects they create: letter writing, list-making, and line drawing. In other instances, one does not wish to create an entirely new object. Rather, writing can also aim to reproduce an already existing text. Nowadays, copies and replicas are often seen as derivatives.[182] 'Copycat' is not a term of endearment, whereas the 'authentic' object enjoys an unparalleled aura.[183] In Egyptology, as well as in many other fields of textual criticism,[184] one wishes to differentiate corrupt copies from authentic variants in order to reconstruct the original ancient text, the Urtext.[185] Francis Llewellyn Griffith, for example, expressed a hope 'that we might one day discover the hoard of rolls of such a copyist and writer' who is a true expert and not a 'hack' – that is, one with a will to learn ancient texts but limited knowledge.[186]

However, the ancient Egyptian visual culture reveals the inappropriateness of pursuits after an unspoiled original.[187] Artists took inspiration, practised new compositions based on known elements, and created networks of iconographic correspondences.[188] A productive definition is that of a creative re-enactment. Important monuments may have inspired other artists to reuse a motif or a scene composition, and this practice appears both in royal and non-royal contexts. Such inspirations operated locally and within a short time span (for example, New Kingdom Thebes), or transregionally (among New Kingdom Elkab, Thebes, Memphis),[189] and over longer periods of time.[190] As a result, 'all representational artistic work in ancient Egypt can be understood to a certain extent as "performance"'.[191]

Similarly, most of the Egyptian written culture calls for a more flexible understanding of the copying process.[192] 'Classics' were copied, but each

---

[182] In philology and literary studies, this view was strong and critiqued vocally only in 1999 by Bernard Cerquiglini.

[183] As Walter Benjamin eloquently noted in his *The Work of Art in an Age of Mechanical Reproduction*.

[184] Burkard 1977; Graefe and van Voss 1993.   [185] A view critiqued by Parkinson 2009: 241.

[186] Griffith and Bradbury Griffith 1917: 5229.

[187] Laboury 2017: 247. Compare the critique of this approach for texts by Quirke 2004.

[188] Laboury 2017: 240–1.   [189] Den Doncker 2017; Laboury 2017.

[190] See, for example, Arnold 2008 or Manuelian 1993: 1–58, among others.

[191] Arnold 2008: 8–9.   [192] Scalf 2016: 204.

copy reflected the copyist's interpretation of the text and its language.[193] If we adopt this perspective of a continuous life of a text, source texts remain essential,[194] but changes and adaptations become as significant, bearing witness to instances of reading and a multitude of uses.[195] In these pursuits, the copyist is viewed as an actor in a cultural network that engages people, artifacts, and sites.[196] Consider, for example, a copyist who wrote down (probably from memory) a selection from literary texts (for example, an instruction or wisdom text) in a tomb (as in Assiut tomb N13.1[197]). He used a text that carried critical cultural values as a witness to his ability to understand and write, leaving this personal testimony in a place he believed to be meaningful.

Recent decades began to recognize the other mechanisms at play.[198] Copying may carry various purposes[199] and functions within reproductive and productive traditions.[200] Productive or open traditions adapt in interaction with social and historical circumstances. Reproductive or closed traditions are embedded in a specific historical moment and passed down as accurately as possible.

As ancient texts and images are copied by hand, often a creative interpretation is produced since exact word-by-word reproductions are not always achieved or even deemed crucial. In addition, practices of replicating texts were widespread in ancient Egypt, yet their boundaries remain fuzzy. On one hand, literary compositions maintained their vigour through their copies,[201] while on the other, copying was done on a daily basis to replicate the contents of reports, accounts, and other documents. Moreover, texts could be multiplied, adapted, and quoted, while styles and registers could be taken up or emulated.[202] Throughout these different practices, the mechanics of copying varies greatly while opening up, in many of its instances, similar discursive spaces that acknowledge a relationship: between original and copy as well as past and present.[203]

---

[193] Parkinson 2009: 207 f.   [194] Compare Backes 2011, also Quack 2011.

[195] Inspired by the important work of Cerquiglini. For similar inquiries in medieval history, see Griffin and Purcell 2018. Emphatically recommended for Egyptian context by Parkinson 2002: 50, Quirke 2004, and Geoga 2021.

[196] We use this term in the sense of Latour's (2005) ANT; its use for historical cultures was discussed, for example, by Hodder 2012. See Assmann 1999.

[197] For an edition of the literary texts from this tomb in Assiut, see Verhoeven 2020.

[198] Compare Briggs and Burke 2020: 25–30.

[199] However, the possibility 'daß bei verschiedenen Gattungen der Literatur durchaus verschiedene Tradierungsarten anzutreffen sind' was seen clearly by Burkard 1977: 4, and distinction of the purposes for copying the classical text is made passim, especially 319–20.

[200] Discussed in Assmann 1983: 7–12, and see further contributions in Gillen 2017.

[201] See Simon 2013: 227–81, with overview of previous literature.

[202] Hoey 2005; Gillen 2014. For an overview of quotes from literary texts, see Manuelian 1993: 1; for reception of select texts, see Parkinson 2009.

[203] Quirke 2004a: 30.

5.1 Copying As Training

Copies could be made for one's training[204] and for professional education,[205] but copies of diverse texts, from royal eulogies to dream books, and from novels to medical texts – such as in the library of the Deir el-Medina scribe Qenherkhepeshef and his family (the Chester Beatty papyri) – were collected by advanced professionals throughout a lifetime or across several generations.[206]

Within one's professional education, copying could serve as an essential method.[207] Trainee scribes could write to dictation, with a model text in front of them, or even from memory.[208] The resulting copies – often those of the literary texts – were also checked, with so-called verse points (red, occasionally black dots) possibly signifying parts of the text were reviewed,[209] or marked as units for recitation.[210] While copying, apprentices could better grasp orthography, script, and turns of phrase. However, the long life of the Egyptian culture and the continuity in the use and reproduction of texts present greater challenges. Copying *Sinuhe* in the New Kingdom was a task not entirely dissimilar to excerpting the first edition of Shakespeare by a modern English speaker. Especially in the Ramesside period, when the written language of daily use was Late Egyptian, copyists working with a Middle Egyptian text must have felt some distance.[211]

Therefore, the copyist's intent is often hard to discern from the copy itself. Many copies might seem imperfect in our eyes; some indeed represent a phase in the training process, still within and for education. Others could be made by those whose professional life never required them to master all the nuances of precision and calligraphy.[212] The latter example may be applicable in Deir el-Medina, a community with higher-than-average literacy but not a community of professional administrators or trained calligraphers.[213] In many instances, by copying a literary text, one makes a claim of its continued applicability of its contents, language, or script.[214]

---

[204] Burkard (1977: 316–22) identified different kinds of variations or 'mistakes' that might have been caused by different copying processes, such as dictation or transcript, for example. In his view, these are often errors, but he also acknowledged the possibility of a textual variant, and he certainly recognized diverse reasons for copying – from training to transmission.

[205] See Parkinson 2009: 205–7; there is a debate as to the organization of the education of scribes from Walle 1963 to McDowell 1996 and Ragazzoli 2019.

[206] Ragazzoli 2019: 156–60.   [207] Burkard 1977.   [208] Goelet 2008, 2015.

[209] On which see further Goelet 2008, 2015.   [210] Parkinson 2009: 184.

[211] See Parkinson 2009: 277–8, and, more recently, Geoga forthcoming.

[212] A term Briggs and Burke also used in the context of degrees of literacy in different cultures; see Briggs and Burke 2020.

[213] Compare Janssen 1992 and Osing 1997.

[214] Parkinson 2009; exemplified further in Parkinson and Spencer 2017.

5.2 Copying As Accounting

Copying numbers for accounts required accuracy and enabled it by copying from a written *Vorlage*. These originals might have been disposed of afterwards or stored separately from the resulting clean copy as duplicates.[215] Letters were copied, perhaps to allow the sender to archive their copy,[216] while institutional archives kept copies of letters relating to the daily business (Middle Kingdom letters from Illahun or the documents probably stored in *ḥtm* ('the enclosure') at Deir el-Medina).[217] Copies of relevant documents were enclosed in legal cases archived by various organizations, including the bureau of the vizier.[218]

Jaroslav Černý proposed that in the New Kingdom, a short-term record on ostraca would be copied to a longer-term record on papyrus. According to his interpretation, the masses of ostraca from Deir el-Medina point to a well-defined administrative practice. Ostraca could also be marked with *spḫr*, 'to copy, to register, or to process' to indicate they were 'processed' in the administration.[219]

While the preservation of papyri or ostraca may be coincidental,[220] current corpora of ostraca and papyri portray a more complex interrelationship.[221] In some cases, ostraca were indeed drafts or mother copies for records on papyri. In other instances, a draft could be made directly on papyrus and then washed off and replaced by a clean copy. In addition, using drafts does not mean that a wholly drafted text must have been adjusted into a clean copy. Drafts could have also contained superfluous information that was no longer needed later in the administrative process – this type of copying was selective, for example, to compile a final account or list of supplies.[222] Not all draft information would be duplicated for the purpose of a clean copy.

While copying requires a more nuanced approach, Černý's analysis still raises valid points about drafts. The use of draft ostraca represents a specific form of text transmission, also extending well beyond administrative use: it is likely that, for example, long hieroglyphic texts on tomb walls were copied from draft ostraca.[223] At least in some settings, western Thebes being a case in point, there could have been a tendency to diversify writing (and yet again also drawing) materials according to their practical use.[224]

---

[215] Donker van Heel and Haring 2003; Eyre 2013.

[216] Summarized for the Deir el-Medina production in Donker van Heel and Haring 2003.

[217] Luft 2006: pBerlin 10096, pBerlin 10045; Eyre 2013: 233–52.   [218] Eyre 2013: 261 f.

[219] Wb 4, 106.11–107.6; FCD 223; Lesko, Dictionary, III, 40) (TLA lemma–no. 133040).

[220] Discussed in detail in Donker van Heel and Haring 2003, Writing, part i.

[221] Haring 2020.   [222] Donker van Heel and Haring 2003: 38.

[223] Haring 2015; Lüscher 2015.   [224] See also Haring 2020.

The bureaucratic process relied on duplication and preservation of records but could also be subverted and undermined by their destruction or absence.[225] The apocalyptic lament of Ipuwer in the *Dialogue with the Lord of All* emphasizes that: 'O, yet the sacred forehall, its writings have been removed', 'office<s> have been opened and th<eir> inventories removed', and indeed 'O, yet scribes of the field-register, their writings have been obliterated'.[226] The lament notes different areas where writing was deployed to serve purposes of social hierarchy and (elite) culture: cultural, 'sacred,' texts, inventories, and accounts, all affected by wanton destruction.

5.3 Copying As Collecting

Some advancing scribes chose to create a personal library of texts they might have copied for themselves.[227] This practice is well illustrated in the New Kingdom's Ramesside text production, exemplified by the *Late Egyptian Miscellanies*,[228] which attest to a flourishing practice of personal selections of texts by dedicated scribes. These *Miscellanies* are collections of texts primarily written on papyri, with some short specimens or selections also on ostraca. They were produced across Ramesside Egypt and contain model letters, teachings, eulogies, model administrative material (reports), and select religious texts.[229] The tradition of teachings that promote the scribal profession itself goes back to the *Teaching of Khety*, likely a Middle Kingdom text, followed by New Kingdom copyists and epigons, which introduced a picturesque comparison of all other jobs laden with toil and discomfort with the managerial role of the 'scribe', a literate organizer of other people's tasks. The exceptionality of writing as a cultural tool, the privileged tool of memory, culminates in a Late Egyptian text known as the *Immortality of the Writer*, on P. Chester Beatty IV, one of the *Ramesside Miscellanies* papyri.

Within the miscellanies, approaches to copying diversified into open and closed copying,[230] in which texts might have been duplicated or adapted.[231] The personal texts collections were likely linked to a double interest of the compilator: his professional involvement with texts and his (or even his family's) personal interests.[232] Surviving papyri and writing boards suggest these

---

[225] Eyre 2013: 'Process, Storage, Record'.

[226] See Enmarch 2008, 227–8 (commentary on pp. 118–19). The text has a considerable New Kingdom reception (p. 25).

[227] Though one could consider it a double library containing also the texts they knew or knew about, akin to Foucault's 'virtual archive'; see Webb 2012: 117.

[228] Ragazzoli 2017a and 2019.

[229] Ragazzoli overview 2017a and 2019 edition: Gardiner 1937, translation and commentary Caminos 1954.

[230] See also Backes 2011: 463–7.   [231] Parkinson 2002: 52–5; Ragazzoli 2017a.

[232] Blumenthal 2011.

practices existed earlier,[233] and although the *Miscellanies* – in the form known from the Ramesside period – disappeared in the Third Intermediate Period, text collecting and archiving continued, including the creation of libraries and archives.[234] The textual production – and probably also storage – expanded further in the New Kingdom and the first millennium:[235] 'Grouping of texts in finds and their long-term survival show something of the value ascribed to them. Occasional texts migrated from being context bound … the most striking instances are copies of early Classical Egyptian Asyut biographical texts in Tebtunis papyri.'[236]

Another aspect of copying involved the concerns of the audience.[237] Within religious and funerary contexts, an experienced copyist might have decided to select, adapt, or modify a text.[238] Some cultural and religious texts had a particularly complex life in this respect. Some copies were made for more restricted purposes, such as fulfilling a ritual role in the cult, whether divine, royal, or funerary,[239] but also ordered by an individual with individual concerns. Dedicated scribes were trained in the netherworld literature.[240]

Almost any major religious collection had variants. *Pyramid texts* are not the same in each pyramid, ditto coffin texts collections, which differ from artifact to artifact. The *Book of the Dead* was bound to contain a fixed selection of essential chapters, but it was a varying collection of both textual and visual material, and 'each manuscript is individual: no two are identical'.[241] The religious text production shows adaptability. For long periods of time, there were no canonical collections with a completely strictly defined content. What mattered was the efficacy of the text collection in assuring a functional transition into the afterlife. Some copies act as reference books more than as complete textual collections, as spells in the *Book of the Dead* could be abbreviated without losing their functionality and efficacy.[242] As the repertory of religious textual corpus grew, the reproductive tradition took on new dimensions and textual production drew on archives, libraries, and possibly even extant monuments.[243] Eventually, the *Book of the Dead* obtained a relatively fixed, canonical sequence in the so-called Saite Recension.[244]

This widespread circulation required dedicated workshops that produced the *Book of the Dead* from the New Kingdom onwards, using specialists trained in

---

[233] Simon 2013: 225; Hagen 2019b.   [234] Hagen 2019a.   [235] Fischer-Elfert 2017.

[236] Baines 2003, 9; see further Kahl 1999: 268–70.   [237] Parkinson 2002: 52.

[238] The modification could have operated multidimensionally in lexical but also orthographic strategies; see Chantrain and Di Biase-Dyson 2017.

[239] Kahl and von Falck 2000: 216; see also Assmann 1983a: 7–8.   [240] Goelet 2010.

[241] Taylor 2010: 13, 55–6.   [242] Taylor 2010: 31–2.   [243] Kahl and von Falck 2000.

[244] Taylor 2010: 58.

cursive hieroglyphs and archaizing hieratic.[245] But copying religious texts also contained the element of producing diverse selections for specimens used in ritual and funerary practice. Here, adapting for an audience might have played a role. A knowledgeable individual could have wished for a specific ritual text collection within the framework of suitable and efficacious texts.[246]

Other netherworld-related texts (apart from the aforementioned collections, there was an entire library of netherworld literature) were selected and organized in tailored collections, possibly with the involvement of the future user.[247] Padiamenope, a Late Period dignitary in Thebes, was proud of having collected a whole library of significant texts in his tomb,[248] creating a realm of knowledge alongside a realm of memory.[249] Saite shaft tombs in the Memphite area demonstrate a similarly rich corpus that recombined elements of previously known funerary texts in an innovative way.[250] This sort of excerpting and copying required expertise in both hieroglyphic and hieratic scripts and was likely the domain of specialist scribes attached to the Egyptian temples. The efficacy of the text that secured a good afterlife was of paramount interest.

5.4 Claiming Copies

The copyist of a *Book of the Dead* would be a zh^3 $sphr$, the same term that marks copied administrative as 'processed'. The role of the word goes further: $sphr$ features frequently in the so-called colophons, statements at the end of the text which indicate the writer's name, commitment, and integrity of the text.[251] A colophon of a spell in a *Book of the Dead* might also refer to its correct use or 'provide a recommendation for its efficacy'.[252] In some cases, the text's integrity was articulated as nothing added or subtracted, potentially suggesting a quality demand on the copyist that would indicate some reflection on the 'corruption' potential of copying.[253]

The role of a colophon in literary or cultural texts is more comprehensive than only marking a successfully copied text specimen. A colophon could be dedicated to others and to divine beings, reflecting the importance of the text and its transmission. It is a personal commemorative monument to the scribe, linking the writer to his colleagues. Texts are copied by someone, but also *for* someone – and to the god, Thoth, making the successfully written text a particular sort of offering:[254] 'for the

---

[245] Goelet 2010.   [246] Landgrafova 2015.

[247] Recently Gestermann 2005, Landgrafova 2015, and Morales 2017.   [248] Traunecker 2014.

[249] Compare Cancik-Kirschbaum and Kahl 2018, the terminology of a 'Wissensort' (pp. 104–5).

[250] Illustrated on Abusir by Landgrafova 2015.

[251] Simon 2013: 253–60. See also Hagen 2012: 97 f.   [252] Taylor 2010: 32.

[253] Quirke 2004a: 30.   [254] Ragazzoli 2019: 518–23.

scribe and master of writing, who gives an office to whom he loves, Thoth, lord of Hermopolis,(and for) the scribe Nekhi ... '[255]

The importance of colophons as personal commemoration is emphasized by their use in secondary epigraphy.[256] A tomb dipinto that took the format of a colophon is a written monument to the literato left in an important location. For instance, a scribe, Khaemwese, in Asyut praised Thoth and focused on his own literacy and ability in a colophon before following up with the offering formula.[257] Instead of the statement of presence and engagement with the visited sacred space of the shrine (which was the common content of visitors' texts in tombs), the colophon text focused on the scribe.

Claiming copies could also take place across discursive spaces and media. Like Rawer in the Old Kingdom (see Section 1), other elite men chose to monumentalize missives from the king, carving them on their monuments, temple walls, and stelae. For example, the Eighteenth Dynasty Nubian viceroy Usersatet included a 'copy of the royal decree' – *mj.tj wḏ* on a stela that depicts him offering gold to the king (Boston MFA 25.632). Usersatet speaks of a royal command and advice that was made by the king himself: 'What the king prepared with his own hands' (see Section 1). The parallelism between the stela and a related text from the shrine in the Nubian site of Ibrim suggests that Amenhotep II may initially have spoken the text,[258] and therefore, the act of copying was repeated twice: from spoken to written and from papyrus to stone. Whatever role the original document might have had, this role was expanded with its new materialization on private tomb walls or monumental stelae, the materialization that is reflected in the document itself.[259] Having a copy of a royal document inbuilt into one's biographical self-thematization reflected a close and special relationship of the dignitary to the king and their shared discourse of legitimation and authority.[260]

5.5 Concluding Remarks

It is appealing to see *sphr* as a causative verb derived from *phr* ꜣ꞉, 'to circulate'.[261] This verb, however, is closely related to the Egyptian magical practice, an important magical term that articulates the practice of magic by the

[255] Posener 1950: 72–4; Ragazzoli 2019: 520.   [256] Verhoeven 2020: 226–30, 315–16.

[257] Verhoeven 2020: 39.   [258] Darnell 2014: 249.

[259] Compare Stauder-Porchet 2021b: 145 (and on Usersatet see, p. 163).

[260] Baines 1997 uses the Old Kingdom example; see also in detail Stauder-Porchet 2021a and 2021b, with the emphasis on the royal inscription as a gift to the dignitary.

[261] umhergehen; umwenden; zirkulieren; umgeben; durchziehen Wb 1, 544.12–547.7; Wilson, Ptol. Lexikon, 366 f.

rite of circumambulation; *phr* thus becomes 'to encircle, to control, to enchant', and *phr.t* a 'remedy'.[262]

The 'circulation' hiding behind *sphr* would help to explain why it is often used in colophons, indicating that a text was correctly copied and, therefore, in practical terms, another version of it entered the circulation. A copy enables a text, giving it further life and pertinence that is not limited to providing information to a new generation of readers. P. Chester Beatty IV indicates that writing's magical power (*hk3*) touches all who read wisdom texts.[263]

The powers evoked by *sphr* differ from – and overlap with – those evoked by 'copy', a term which ultimately derives from the name of the Roman goddess of abundance, Copia (her name is reflected in the name of the cornucopia, a symbol of abundance), surviving, for example, in English and Italian expressions for 'abundant, plentiful' – *copious, copioso*.[264] This expression evoked notions of resources, power, or plenty, and continued to do so until the Renaissance. The Egyptian *sphr* might have indicated a similar concept of resources recreated, made plentiful and powerful by copying.

The vocabulary used for transcribing, copying, and recording suggests a self-aware, reflective approach to duplicating and copying. Their overlaps and differences seem to have been acknowledged to some degree in the administrative and literary practice. In its different implementations: copying at work, copying for yourself, for the community, for the past, and for the future, copying signifies transmitting culture and being human in interaction with your world. The intellectual and material practice of copying enabled first training and then the development of scribal practice. Copying was an exercise that allowed both the survival of texts and their ongoing actualization and appropriation. In that respect, Egyptian copying was a productive, vigorous practice that kept both training and text-making in motion. The Egyptian literati could have approved of some elements of Marcus Boon's 'praise of copying',[265] but theirs was not a practice that would appear as limited to the subaltern or dispossessed, but a practice intended to keep the Egyptian culture, including the high elite culture, in operation.

6 Reading

Reading and *writing* often seem like two equal parts of the writing culture. However, while the two overlap in certain social contexts, they inhabit very different forms in others. The difference between the two is even starker when one considers our own field, Egyptology, and its relationship with ancient texts

---

[262] Ritner 1993: 2.   [263] See Simon 2013: 269 regarding P. Chester Beatty IV vso 3,9 f.
[264] Boon 2010: 41–7.   [265] Boon 2010.

and modern publications. Key to these entanglements, as we show in what follows, is the figure of the 'scribe' set within the network of the ancient society and culture. We will sketch the outlines of historical Egyptological readings as a starting point for further considerations. We have deliberately changed the perspective from ancient texts and practitioners to the scholars and writers of the modern era, who try to understand the ancient culture. In doing so, they create yet another network of texts, mediating the reading of the ancient lives that were so involved in both reading and writing.

6.1 Practitioners with Concealed Baggage?

The figure of the 'scribe' is omnipresent in the Egyptological literature, as he appears to be in the Egyptian record. Sometimes he has been expressly identified with a literato, and at other times with a bureaucrat, but the understanding of roles and expectations linked to this title was diversified only implicitly (as were Egyptian text genres).[266]

Stephen Quirke called 'scribe' a word with 'concealed baggage', comparable to another professional designation, 'priest'.[267] Quirke considered 'scribe', or even a related term 'secretary', to be potentially 'orientalist stereotype', and this view was further developed by Pinarello.[268] As Quirke acknowledges, 'secretary' is not only an administrator or personal assistant, but used to be and still is an administrative or governmental title carrying considerable authority and prestige. Whilst we may identify simplifications,[269] we may also detect more ambivalent observations in Egyptological literature which articulate relatable preoccupations with the limits of our understanding. The selections that follow only skim the surface of the complex relationship of Egyptologists and Egyptian writing hands.

John Gardner Wilkinson addressed many aspects of Egyptian life in his *Manners and Customs of Ancient Egyptians*. He opened his narrative with a requirement of historian's impartiality – by placing Egypt in the East (creating a sense of detachment), but asking for a non-judgemental openness to the customs of others: 'to judge impartially of their character, we must examine the comparative state of other neighbouring and contemporary nations, and measure it by the standard of the era in which they lived … avoid as much as possible the invidious comparison of European and Oriental manners'.[270] His understanding of the Egyptian society was very much in debt of classical authors and operated with the concept of 'castes'. Interestingly, he and his

---

[266] See Lesko 1994. Compare Berlev 1997, Velde 1986. Examples include Quirke 2004a and 2004b; for an outline of literary studies, see Loprieno 2001 and Baines 2003.

[267] Quirke (2004b: 15–16) argued extensively and critically against an uncritical use.

[268] Pinarello 2015.   [269] Baines 2003.   [270] Wilkinson 1878: I, v.

classical informers did not place 'scribes' into a role of a separate caste. Wilkinson argued that 'royal scribes' were among the highest echelons of society, whereas 'notaries' were grouped with builders as well as boatmen.[271] However problematic the restrictive concept of 'castes' was, literacy was still seen as cutting across its barriers adding a vertical link in horizontal strata. Gaston Maspero noted by 1895 that 'the title of a scribe does not mean anything by itself'[272] – the literate person needed to be seen in context to understand their position and significance.[273]

For Adolf Erman, the scribes 'set up an ideal of the official, which possesses some elements of greatness. The official is to be impartial, one who protects the insignificant against the powerful; the clever person who knows a way out even in the midst of greatest difficulties; the humble one, who never thrusts himself forward, and yet whose opinion is heard in the council'.[274] Erman paraphrased the instruction texts, preferring their voice over his own, achieving a reflection of the Egyptian ethics concerned with authority and power.

Gardiner distinguished, using his characteristic – and, on occasion, acidic – writing style, diverse practitioners of writing in Egypt. On one end of the imaginary literacy and skill gauge stood authors of instructions and *onomastica* like Amenemope, intellectuals holding 'the laudable view that a man is never too old to learn'[275] (even though Gardiner thought the *Onomasticon* to be 'tedious'[276]), and making writing style choices 'consciously adopting an archaistic style or else unconsciously employing forms from early manuscripts he had previously copied'. He also appreciated 'a skilled professional' who 'used an experienced business style'[277] in the Turin Strike Papyrus. His assessments most likely united a wish to provide an objective description of an official document written in a legible and well-organized hand with his own subjectivity of a transcriber – more legible documents are easier to work with.

On the other end of the gauge, there might have been the draughtsmen of Deir el-Medina, in whose abilities Gardiner facetiously professed to his colleague Černý to have but little trust: '[W]hat can you expect of these degenerate Necropolis workmen? I don't know whether they are worse when they are copying unintelligibly some good old literary texts or when they are writing about their own affairs!'[278] The addressee of this note, Černý, identified the ambiguity of 'scribes' in the community of Deir el-Medina: draughtsmen and administrators could be both defined (or self-defined) as 'scribes'.[279] He saw them as connected, indeed contiguous, in terms of social mobility (and skill),

---

[271] Wilkinson 1878: I, 157–8.   [272] Maspero 1895: I, 287–8.   [273] Pinarello 2015: 20–1.
[274] Erman 1927: xxviii.   [275] Gardiner 1947: I, 5.   [276] Gardiner 1947: I, 25.
[277] Gardiner 1948: xvi.   [278] GIA, Collection Černý, Černý Mss. 21.778, 9 February 1950.
[279] Černý 1973: 191–3.

with only the 'scribes of the tomb' linked by administration and in contact with high state officials. He also used the word *scribe* in quotation marks on some occasions, including in popular writings,[280] adding explanatory notes. He also approached the 'scribes' of Deir el-Medina as a group of individuals with the potential to elucidate individual literary interests and writing styles, as well as their social network.[281]

In the 1980s/90s, Oleg Berlev took a bird's-eye view of the legacy of the scribes and suggested that the reputation of the Egyptian bureaucracy as a large and well-oiled apparatus eventually influenced the reception of Egypt. Berlev's view uses the ancient projection of the status of Egyptian literati. He chose to illustrate this specific feature not by only the classical legacy of Egyptian wisdom (Herodotus), but also in the biblical story of Joseph. Here the administrator/manager rises to a figure of heroic proportions: 'bureaucracy is depicted as a colossal force, capable of withstanding an unrelenting nature and of transforming the socioeconomic structure of a people of many millions'.[282]

Eyre, although disagreeing with the efficiency and centrality of Egypt's bureaucracy' proposed that 'There were not distinct classes of person, but simply more or less learned members of the same literate class of office holders, whose greater personal learning might reflect their access to more prestigious and profitable offices ... a single, culturally homogeneous group of scribes.'[283]

In some recent compendia, the 'scribes' are not highlighted as a particular social group, but literacy is presented as a function of state administration or culture in the hands of diverse practitioners.[284] Current studies in New Kingdom scribal culture[285] propose that the 'scribe'/*zẖꜣ* is an ancient Egyptian label with a functional (not perfect) translation and a polyvalent reading which the Egyptological interpretation needs to specify contextually. It is noticeable that the interpretations differ in terms of homogeneity attributed or denied to 'scribes', with a large part of our knowledge based on the projections of scribal status in the Middle Kingdom and especially in the New Kingdom.

These select examples are only a limited sample of evidence, but they suggest that a rather more nuanced picture is emerging in the Egyptological literature than that of 'illusory creatures'[286] with an orientalizing label. These very different 'scribes' may be interpreted as part of the elite or sub-elite, some of them quite humble. There is some discussion about how complex or layered the Egyptian society might have been,[287] but people with varying degrees of

---

[280] Černý 1929.   [281] Černý 1973: 193–230.   [282] Berlev 1997: 87.   [283] Eyre 2013: 352.
[284] See Lloyd 2010, especially Allen 2010.   [285] Allon and Navratilova 2017; Ragazzoli 2019.
[286] Pace Pinarello 2015: 21.   [287] Frood 2010.

literacy might well have been present across a significant part of the Egyptian society.[288] The scholars did not strip 'the social category of "scribe" of any performative role until it became reified in the fetishized artefact types of pen and writing palette'.[289]

Finally, there is still an assumed or existing ambiguity in the relationship of the practitioners of Egyptology to the practitioners of the art and craft of writing in ancient Egypt. Quirke, interested in the 'orientalist' lens, noted that 'the "scribe" represents the enemy of enlightenment scholarship, a medieval or oriental sloth in administration, and a bumbling and incompetent copyist'.[290] Yet Egyptological images of a scribe have often been vivid, inspired by Ramesside miscellanies, including Egyptological narratives enchanted by Egyptian poetry or captivated by length of tradition. Egyptologists identify[291] or are identified with the scribes. The social world of scribes and the academic world resonate.[292] Perhaps this latter approach may help in achieving the balance of detachment and affinity that is required in the historian's craft.

6.2 Scripts, Texts, Literature, Reading

The history of reflections on the Egyptian scribe in Egyptology (including before professional Egyptology of the nineteenth to the twenty-first centuries) is intertwined with thoughts on the complexity and qualities of Egyptian scripts and literature, and on writing as a technique and as a tool of cultural communication.

For texts, the Egyptological approach has long preferred, by necessity and by paradigm, an editorial activity over an interpretive one. '"Understanding" succumbs more easily to the ravages of time than "editing."'[293] This is noticeable in the study of the Egyptian literature,[294] which has been read to achieve modern synoptic editions (making the text or a textual composite accessible), but not necessarily read *with* the multiplicity of *its ancient audiences*.[295] Earlier evaluations of ancient cultural communications did not equal the analytical approach expected in more recent research.[296]

The Egyptian writing system resonated in many narratives, inside and outside Egypt, and for some, Egypt became its hieroglyphs.[297] Byzantine scholars used hieroglyphic writing as an interpretive framework for the *Iliad*.[298] Foremost Islamic scholars attempted to read hieroglyphs centuries before they became

[288] Janssen 1992.   [289] Thus Pinarello 2015: 147.   [290] Quirke 2004b: 15.
[291] Quirke 2004b: 50.   [292] Ragazzoli 2019: 145.
[293] Assmann 1995: 4. On a recommended Egyptological practice, see Quack 2011.
[294] Baines 2003.   [295] Parkinson 2009 has extensively pursued this perspective.
[296] As outlined by Loprieno 2001 and Baines 2003.
[297] For late antique reception, see Westerfeld 2019.   [298] Morenz 2022.

a Renaissance fascination.[299] Both medieval and Renaissance scholars had an active interest in hieroglyphs as symbols of a venerable culture.[300] Following Latin translations of the *Corpus Hermeticum* and of Plato in the fifteenth century, a search for the original wisdom of Egypt intensified in Europe. Hieroglyphs were of interest as a symbolic code, as a supposed guiding principle of emblematic encoding,[301] and as a symbol for the possibility of finding a perfect language.[302] Yet the European views on Hermes Trismegistos and alleged Egyptian traditions soon encompassed ambivalence that gradually extended to most Western perceptions of Egypt. If the Enlightenment saw Egypt as a culture that had much to offer to the contemporary man, the Romantic view found an assumed darker side.[303] One intellectual, Johann Wolfgang von Goethe, who stood between Enlightenment and romanticism, encapsulated this change by his own volte-face: '[I]n his late years, Egyptian antiquity and Indian and Chinese as well, were "ever mere curiosities; it is good to make oneself and the world familiar with them; but they bear scant fruit for moral and aesthetic training."'[304] At a glance, this quote might seem to illustrate the postcolonial point of the 'European man at the centre of an oriental panopticon',[305] the European or Western self classifying and edifying the rest of the world by its presence and control. Yet the European involvement with other cultures, distant in time or in space, is, like most cultural contacts, intricate.[306] Next to and intertwined with geopolitical dimensions there was always an intellectual and emotional involvement where awe and control mixed, often uneasily. A will to categorize and label other humans was challenged by the search for a shared humanity.[307]

As evolutionary views, influenced by Charles Darwin, Jean Baptiste Lamarck, and their followers, gained traction, past cultures (own or other) and their manifestations were also seen as steps on the journey of human evolution.[308] These views supported an assessment of a complicated, pre-alphabetical script system, and a vision of a more 'primitive' writing or languages as something to expect in antiquity. The views on ancient Egypt were developing in this context:

> It was in the 1870s and 1880s, not in the 1820s or 1830s, that the impact of decipherment really began to make its presence felt and it was in the 1870s, not in the Napoleonic era, that Egyptologists found ways to communicate

---

[299] See Daly 2005, but see also reviews in Jakeman 2005 and Colla 2008; an outline focused on reception and appreciation of hieroglyphs is provided by Sundermeyer 2020.

[300] See, for example, Iversen 1961 and Jirásková 2020.

[301] Hornung 2001: 83–91; Winand 2022. For the sake of completeness, Egyptian enigmatic or cryptograhic writing must be mentioned; see Klotz and Stauder 2020.

[302] Eco 1995.   [303] Hornung 2001: 137.   [304] Hornung 2001: 131.   [305] Pinarello 2015: 16.

[306] MacKenzie 1995: 213–15.

[307] Osterhammel 2015. For visual culture, also see Edwards 2012, 2015; Lydon et al. 2016.

[308] Fasolo 2012.

directly with the public and began to gain sustained interest and support ...
Most importantly of all, it was in these late nineteenth-century decades that
the developing meanings of ancient Egypt began to be rooted deep ...
through their association with issues as culturally provocative as the nature
of the Old Testament, the cultural status of classical literature, and the
viability of evolution (Darwinian and otherwise).[309]

Egyptology had 'professionalized' alongside many other sciences and
humanities disciplines, throughout the nineteenth century. It had to negotiate
its own status in a panoply of disciplines and its position in society.[310] The
latter task led to a continuous engagement with a wider social and cultural
debate, including with its controversial aspects.[311] In the second half of the
nineteenth century, the paradigm of philological priority in Egyptology put
Egypt 'in the shadow of texts',[312] so to a certain extent in the shadow of the
scribe.

What followed was a fitting of the Egyptians, including their literati, on
a comparative scale of cultural competence and intellectual insight with
other nations. Yet Egyptologists had ambivalent feelings about their own
adequacy in assessing the writing, literacy, and literature of the ancient
Egyptians. Often, an appeal of humanity shared by the modern and ancient
peoples was invoked. In 1906, Battiscombe Gunn offered a fascinating
insight into Ptahhotep as an ever-relevant reader of human characters: '[I]t
is as fresh and readable as in the year after it was written. Will the books of
our time last one-tenth so long?'[313] Nathaniel Reich chafed against the force
of the philological paradigm. Fascinated with the possibility of studying an
ancient mind, he was critical of Wilhelm Spiegelberg's approach: 'S. has –
as I will prove it – not even a limited understanding of a psychology of an
Egyptian scribe.'[314]

Not everyone was convinced of the relevance of such an appeal. Francis
Llewellyn and Kate Griffith claimed in 1917:

> The advance that has been made in recent years in the decipherment of the
> ancient writings of the world enables us to deal in a very matter-of-fact way
> with the Egyptian inscriptions. Their chief mysteries are solved, their
> philosophy is almost fathomed, their general nature is understood. The
> story they have to tell is seldom startling to the modern mind. The world
> was younger when they were written. The heart of man was given to devious
> ways then, as now and in the days of Solomon, – that we can affirm full well;
> but his mind was simpler: apart from knowledge of men and the conduct of

---

[309] Gange 2013: 1–2.   [310] Bednarski 2020; Bednarski, Dodson, and Ikram 2021.
[311] For instance, the case of Flinders Petrie; see Challis 2013.
[312] Gange 2013. See also Wengrow 2020.   [313] Gunn 1906: 26–7 (quote on p. 26).
[314] Gertzen and Oerter 2017: 22; translated from German by HN.

affairs, the educated Egyptian had no more subtlety than a modern boy of fifteen, or an intelligent English rustic of a century ago.[315]

Gardiner was involved in a detailed study of the *Tale of Sinuhe*, and only this text passed in his eyes as a world classic among the Egyptian literary works.[316]

> I maintain that for us too the Story of Sinuhe is and must remain a classic. It is a classic because it marks a definite stage in the history of the world's literature; and it is a classic because it displays with inimitable directness the mixed naivete and subtility of the old Egyptian character, its directness of vision, its pomposity, its reverence and its humour.[317]

Erman came to a yet different conclusion:

> [T]hey [Egyptians] still bear a reputation of having been a strange people, ossified and without any proper development. And yet in the earlier millennia of their history the Egyptians were the exact antithesis to this popular conception – a gifted people, intellectually alert, and already awake when other nations still slumbered; indeed, their outlook on the world was as a lively and adventurous as was that of the Greeks thousands of years later.[318]

In 1929, Thomas E. Peet suggested that it may well be to our own shortcomings as modern readers that we may need to look first to understanding the writing, language, and literature, or to appreciating the culture and its practitioners: 'We have never heard or spoken Egyptian; we have not enough material, and what we have is too variable in date to allow any scholar to develop that fine literary sense which alone makes complete appreciation possible.'[319]

From the twentieth-century perspective, the ancient mind had limits and yet it spoke to the modern people. Similarly, both literary efforts and the intellectual standing of the 'scribe' were ambivalent. Peet's critique of limitations of understanding of Egyptian grammar and therefore literature was balanced by his more judgemental statement that the Egyptian texts had no power of 'conjuring with words'.[320]

We may find many more contributions to this kaleidoscope, but the selection here may serve to illustrate the assortment of opinions. For Gunn and Erman, Egyptian literature and culture ultimately expressed, at least in part, 'universal human experience or feeling'. Gardiner or Griffith were erecting a barrier by their evolutionary perspective, whilst Peet noted more explicitly where some of the hurdles lay for an appreciation of Egyptian literature. What most of these

---

[315] Griffith and Bradbury Griffith 1917: 5225.   [316] Gardiner 1916; Parkinson 2002; 12–13.
[317] Gardiner 1916, 164.   [318] Erman 1927, transl. Blackman: xxiii.   [319] Peet 1931: 6.
[320] Peet 1931: 131–2.

researchers did was to consider, more or less in detail, the limits of their own knowledge.

Although interpretive perspectives might have been restricted in comparison to a burgeoning editorial apparatus, a tendency for a 'progressivist'[321] evaluation of the Egyptian culture – starting with evaluation of its literature and literati – influenced several generations of Egyptologists up until the 1960s. 'The theory of Egyptian literature emerged gradually in the 1970s',[322] when 'issues of genre came to a head'.[323] Up until then, the 'study of Egyptian literature followed, explicitly or implicitly, two methodological criteria, it was a) euhemeristic and b) adductive'.[324] The first criterion meant a 'sense that texts were sources for the historian, and were to be regarded as normative representatives of a communal culture rather than as individual cultural artefacts'.[325] The second criterion meant that almost any written evidence apart from administrative could be termed literary.[326] This modern amalgamation of Egyptian written production contributed perhaps to a similarly amalgamated view of the 'scribe'. If many things written could be generic 'literature', then anyone writing might be a generic 'scribe'.

Obviously, Egyptologists did realize the existence of different texts and their pointedly different materiality. Different scripts chosen for non-literary and literary texts are a case in point: they helped Černý, Georges Posener, and Serge Sauneron to begin to make sense of the mass of ostraca in Deir el-Medina. Černý analysed non-monumental resources in his social and economic history study and addressed their characteristic materiality.[327] However, the diversity of textual production (regarding both contents and context), as well as the diversity of writing hands, appeared as not fully and explicitly articulated to differentiate a comprehensive range of practices and people behind the different texts.

Within modern Egyptology, evaluations of Egyptian literature and also Egyptian language and script[328] are analysed in order to develop and support a more self-reflective discipline.[329] John Baines and Antonio Loprieno offered models for defining and analysing Egyptian literature,[330] acknowledging that 'cross-culturally, literature is not amenable to an exact definition'.[331] At the same time, Baines articulated the understanding that Egyptology can and should provide a study of written culture that is at once holistic and nuanced and thus assert 'its position among the humanities'.[332]

---

[321] Baines 2003: 2.   [322] Loprieno 1996: 211.   [323] Baines 2003: 3.
[324] Loprieno 1996: 211.   [325] Parkinson 2009: 5.   [326] Loprieno 2001: 212.
[327] Černý 1931 and 1963.   [328] Including its recording; see Davies and Laboury 2020.
[329] Mathieu 2013.   [330] Loprieno 2001; Baines 2003.   [331] Baines 2003: 4.
[332] Baines 2003: 20.

In his review of the readings of Egyptian literature, Parkinson (2009) analysed a historical process of readings and harmonized the concerns of over-
familiarization and over-othering, proposing that 'the modern reception of these
ancient works has now extended beyond (some) institutional boundaries and
beyond concerns with whatever is biblical, historical, or exotic'.[333]

The volume *Erste Philologien* brought a recognition of a pre-classical interest in writing and analysing language;[334] it addressed inscripturation as
a cultural technique and some of its practitioners as early philologists, whilst
critiquing briefly the conventional character of the designation 'scribe'. Its title
indicates not an equation of the ancient language work with modern philology,
but a recognition of its intellectual interest and capacity.

The tendency of editors or commentators to draw some comparison or
evaluation that would link the ancient text to its present reader is inevitable, if
difficult.[335] We may need to identify and appreciate more clearly the search for
balance among (i) a recognition of specificity of the Egyptian 'past as a foreign
country', (ii) a removal of the exoticist, othering lens applied to view Egypt, and
eventually (iii) the search of the present for answers in the past.[336] Coming full
circle, in later twentieth- and early twenty-first-century Egyptology there is an
enhanced tendency to erect barriers against an 'over-familiarisation' of ancient
Egypt, but also against its 'Orientalization'.[337] At the same time, there is an
ongoing lively wish to see ancient Egypt understood on its own terms, surely,
but still comprehensible and relatable.

---

[333] Parkinson 2009: 270–1.   [334] Cancik-Kirschbaum and Kahl 2018.   [335] Quack 2011: 545.
[336] White 1986: 487.
[337] Thus Pinarello 2015, also Eyre 2013: 1–15, 351; see also Wengrow 2020 for another angle on
recontextualizing past objects and actors.

References

Abdelmoniem, Ahmed H. 2020. 'The Professions and Hierarchy of Nekhebu'. *Journal of the General Union of Arab Archaeologists* 5 (2): 1–28.

Allen, James P. 1992. 'Rē'wer's accident'. In *Studies in Pharaonic Religion and Society in Honour of J. Gwyn Griffiths*, edited by Alan B. Lloyd, 14–20. London: Egypt Exploration Society.

Allen, James P. 2010. 'Language, Scripts, and Literacy'. In *A Companion to Ancient Egypt*, vol. 2, edited by Alan B. Lloyd, 641–62. Chichester: Wiley-Blackwell.

Allen, James P. 2002. *The Heqanakht Papyri*. Publications of the Metropolitan Museum of Art Egyptian Expedition 27. New York: Metropolitan Museum of Art.

Allon, Niv. 2013. 'The Writing Hand and the Seated Baboon: Tension and Balance in Statue MMA 29.2.16'. *Journal of the American Research Center in Egypt* 49: 93–112.

   2019. *Writing, Violence, and the Military: Images of Literacy in Eighteenth Dynasty Egypt (1550–1295 BCE)*. Oxford: Oxford University Press.

   2021. 'Finding a Voice in a Hymn to Ramesses IX (MMA 59.51a, b)'. *Studien zur Altägyptischen Kultur* 50: 1–17.

Allon, Niv, and Hana Navratilova. 2017. *Ancient Egyptian Scribes: A Cultural Exploration*. Bloomsbury Egyptology. London: Bloomsbury Academic.

Altenmüller, Hartwig. 2015. *Zwei Annalenfragmente aus dem frühen Mittleren Reich*. Studien Zur Altägyptischen Kultur, Beihefte 16. Hamburg: Helmut Buske.

Andreu, Guillemette. 2013. *L'Art du contour: Le dessin dans l'Egypte ancienne, cat. exp. (Paris, Musée du Louvre, 2013; Bruxelles, Musée Royaux d'Art et d'Histoire, 2013–2014)*. Paris: Louvre éditions.

Arnold, Dorothea. 2008. 'Egyptian Art: A Performing Art?' In *Servant of Mut: Studies in Honor of Richard A. Fazzini*, edited by Sue H. D'Auria, 1–18. Leiden: Brill.

Assmann, Jan. 1983. *Re und Amun: Die Krise des polytheistischen Weltbilds im Ägypten Der 18.–20. Dynastie*. Orbis Biblicus et Orientalis 51. Freiburg: Universitätsverlag.

   1995. *Egyptian Solar Religion in the New Kingdom: Re, Amun and the Crisis of Polytheism*, translated by Anthony Alcock. London: Kegan Paul International.

1999a. *Ägyptische Hymnen und Gebete*. 2nd ed. Orbis biblicus et orientalis. Freiburg: Universitätsverlag.

Backes, Burkhard. 2011. 'Zur Anwendung der Textkritik in der Ägyptologie: Ziele, Grenzen und Akzeptanz'. In *Methodik und Didaktik in der Ägyptologie: Herausforderungen eines kulturwissenschaftlichen Paradigmenwechsels in den Altertumswissenschaften*, edited by Burkhard Backes, Alexandra Verbovsek, and Catherine Jones, 451–79. Munich: Wilhelm Fink.

Bács, Tamás A. 2011. '" . . . Like Heaven in Its Interior": Late Ramesside Painters in Theban Tomb 65'. In *Proceedings of the Colloquium on Theban Archaeology at the Supreme Council of Antiquities, November 5, 2009*, edited by Zahi Hawass, Tamás A. Bács, and Gábor Schreiber, 33–41. Cairo: Conseil Suprême des antiquités de l'Égypte.

2021. 'A Painter's Version: Amenhotep, Son of Amunnakhte and Pictorial Tradition'. *Journal of Egyptian Archaeology* 107 (1–2): 41–56.

Baines, John. 1983. 'Literacy and Ancient Egyptian Society'. *Man* 18 (3): 572–99.

1997. 'Kingship before Literature: The World of the King in the Old Kingdom'. In *Selbstverständnis und Realität: Akten des Symposiums zur Ägyptischen Königsideologie in Mainz 15.–17.6.1995*, edited by Rolf Gundlach and Christine Raedler, 125–74. Wiesbaden: Harrassowitz.

2003. 'Research on Egyptian Literature: Background, Definitions, Prospects'. In *Egyptology at the Dawn of the Twenty-First Century: Proceedings of the Eighth International Congress of Egyptologists, Cairo, 2000*, vol. 3, edited by Lyla Pinch Brock and Zahi Hawass, 1–26. Cairo: American University in Cairo Press.

2007. 'Ancient Egyptian Concepts and Uses of the Past: Third to Second Millennium Evidence'. In *Visual and Written Culture in Ancient Egypt*, edited by John Baines, 179–201. Oxford: Oxford University Press.

2011a. 'Ancient Egypt'. In *The Oxford History of Historical Writing, Volume 1: Beginnings to AD 600*, edited by Grant Hardy and Andrew Feldherr, 53–75. Oxford: Oxford University Press.

2011b. 'Egyptology and the Social Sciences: Thirty Years On'. In *Methodik und Didaktik in der Ägyptologie: Herausforderungen eines Kulturwissenschaftlichen Paradigmenwechsels in den Altertumswissenschaften*, edited by Burkhard Backes, Alexandra Verbovsek, and Catherine Jones, 573–97. Munich: Wilhelm Fink.

Baines, John, and Peter Lacovara. 2002. 'Burial and the Dead in Ancient Egyptian Society: Respect, Formalism, Neglect'. *Journal of Social Archaeology* 2: 5–36.

Bakir, 'Abd el-Moḥsen. 1970. *Egyptian Epistolography from the Eighteenth to the Twenty-First Dynasty*. Bibliothèque d'étude 48. Cairo: Institut français d'Archéologie orientale.

Barta, Winfried. 1963. *Die altägyptische Opferliste, von der Frühzeit bis zur griechisch-römischen Epoche*. Berlin: BHessling.

1968. *Aufbau und Bedeutung der Altägyptischen Opferformel*. Ägyptologische Forschungen 24. Glueckstadt: J. J. Augustin.

Bazin Rizzo, Laure, Annie Gasse, Frédéric Servajean, and Musée Henri Prades de Montpellier agglomération. 2016. *À l'école des scribes: Les écritures de l'Égypte ancienne*. Cahiers de l'ENIM (CENIM) 15. Cinisello Balsamo: SilvanaEditoriale.

Bednarski, Andrew. 2020. 'The Nature and History of Egyptology'. In *The Oxford Handbook of Egyptology*, edited by Andrew Bednarski, Ian Shaw, and Elizabeth Bloxam, 32–47. Oxford: Oxford University Press.

Bednarski, Andrew, Aidan Dodson, and Salima Ikram. 2021. *A History of World Egyptology*. Cambridge: Cambridge University Press.

Belknap, Robert E. 2004. *The List: The Uses and Pleasures of Cataloguing*. New Haven, CT: Yale University Press.

Berlev, Oleg. 1997. 'Bureaucrats'. In *The Egyptians*, edited by Robert Bianchi, Sergio Donadoni, Thomas Ritter, Anna Lisa Crone, and Charles Lambert, 87–119. Chicago, IL: University of Chicago Press.

Blumenthal, Elke. 2011. 'Privater Buchbesitz im Pharaonischen Ägypten'. In *Bibliotheken im Altertum*, edited by Elke Blumenthal and Wolfgang Schmitz, 51–85. Wiesbaden: Harrassowitz.

Boon, Marcus. 2010. *In Praise of Copying*. Cambridge, MA: Harvard University Press.

Borchardt, Ludwig. 1907. 'Das Dienstgebäude des auswärtigen Amtes unter den Ramessiden'. *Zeitschrift für ägyptische Sprache Und Altertumskunde* 44: 59–61.

1910. *Das Grabdenkmal des Königs Śaȝḥu-Reʿ I: Der Bau. Ausgrabungen der Deutschen Orient-Gesellschaft in Abusir 1902–1908*. Wissenschaftliche Veröffentlichungen der Deutschen Orient-Gesellschaft 14. Leipzig: J. C. Hinrichs.

1937. *Denkmäler des Alten Reiches (außer den Statuen) im Museum von Kairo, Nr. 1295–1808. Teil 1: Text und Tafeln zu Nr. 1295–1541*. Catalogue général des antiquités égyptiennes du Musée du Caire. Berlin: Reichsdruckerei.

Borges, Jorge L. 1962 (1956). *Ficciones*, translated by Anthony Kerrigan. New York: Grove Press.

Bowman, Alan K., and Greg Woolf (eds.). 1994. *Literacy and Power in the Ancient World*. Cambridge: Cambridge University Press.

Briggs, Asa, and Peter Burke. 2020. *A Social History of the Media: From Gutenberg to Facebook*. 4th ed. Cambridge, MA: Polity.

Brovarski, Edward 2001. *The Senedjemib Complex I: The Mastabas of Senedjemib Inti (G 2370), Khnumenti (G 2374), and Senedjemib Mehi (G 2378)*, Giza Mastabas 7. Boston, MA: Art of the Ancient World, Museum of Fine Arts.

Brunner-Traut, Emma. 1990. *Frühformen des Erkennens: am Beispiel Altägyptens*. Darmstadt: Wissenschaftliche Buchgesellschaft.

Burkard, Günter. 1977. *Textkritische Untersuchungen zu Ägyptischen Weisheitslehren des Alten und Mittleren Reiches: Ägyptologische Abhandlungen* 34. Wiesbaden: Harrassowitz.

Callender, Vivienne Gae. 2019. *El-Hawawish: Tombs, Sarcophagi, Stelae. Palaeography*. Paléographie hiéroglyphique 8. Cairo: Institut français d'archéologie orientale.

Caminos, Ricardo A. 1954. *Late-Egyptian Miscellanies*. Brown Egyptological Studies I. London: Oxford University Press.

Cancik, Hubert, Helmuth Schneider, and Christine F. Salazar. 2002. *Brill's New Pauly: Encyclopaedia of the Ancient World*. English ed. Managing editor Christine F. Salazar. Leiden: Brill.

Cancik-Kirschbaum, Eva Christiane. 2018. *Erste Philologien: Archäologie einer Disziplin vom Tigris bis zum Nil*. Tubingen: Mohr Siebeck.

Candea, Matei. 2019. *Comparison in Anthropology: The Impossible Method*. New Departures in Anthropology. Cambridge: Cambridge University Press.

Carruthers, Mary. 2008. *The Book of Memory: A Study of Memory in Medieval Culture*. Cambridge: Cambridge University Press.

Cavell, Stanley. 1979. *The Claim of Reason: Wittgenstein, Skepticism, Morality and Tragedy*. Oxford: Oxford University Press.

Černý, Jaroslav. 1929. 'Dělnictvo ve dtarém Egyptě'. *Orient* 2 (5): 29–31.

    1931. 'Les Ostraca Hiératiques, Leur Intérêt et La Nécessité de Leur Étude'. *Chronique d'Égypte* 6 (12): 212–24.

    1963. 'The Contribution of the Study of Unofficial and Private Documents to the History of Pharaonic Egypt'. In *Le Fonti Indirette Della Storia Egiziana / Les Sources Indirectes de l'histoire Égyptienne / Indirect Sources of Egyptian History / Die Indirekten Quellen Der Ägyptischen Geschichte*, edited by Sergio Donadoni, 31–57. Rome: Centro di studi semitici, Università.

Černý, Jaroslav, Serge Sauneron, and Dominique Valbelle. 1973. *A Community of Workmen at Thebes in the Ramesside Period*. Bibliothèque d'étude 50. Cairo: Institut français d'Archéologie orientale.

Cerquiglini, Bernard. 1999. *In Praise of the Variant: A Critical History of Philology*. Parallax. Baltimore, MD: Johns Hopkins University Press.

Challis, Debbie. 2013. *The Archaeology of Race: The Eugenic Ideas of Francis Galton and Flinders Petrie*. London: Bloomsbury.

Chantrain, Gaëlle. 2014. 'The Use of Classifiers in the New Kingdom: A Global Reorganization of the Classifiers System?' *Lingua Aegyptia* 22: 39–59.

Chantrain, Gaëlle, and Camilla Di Biase-Dyson. 2017. 'Making a Case for Multidimensionality in Ramesside Figurative Language'. *Lingua Aegyptia* 25: 41–66.

Chioffi, Marco, and Giuliana Rigamonti. 2020. *Antico Regno 'i decreti reali' I: decreti del II Pepy: decreto 24 Copto B, decreto 28 Dakhla, decreto dell'Horo Demedjibtaui (decreto Copto R)*. Collana sš wr – il grande scriba 11. Imola: La Mandragora.

Cohen, Henri, and Claire Lefebvre. 2005. *Handbook of Categorization in Cognitive Science*. Amsterdam: Elsevier.

Colla, Elliott. 2008. 'Egyptology: The Missing Millennium, Ancient Egypt in Medieval Arabic Writings'. *International Journal of Middle East Studies* 40 (1): 135–7.

Contardi, Federico. 2016. 'The Emergence of Writing and the Construction of Cultural Memory in Egypt'. In *Envisioning the Past through Memories: How Memory Shaped Ancient Near Eastern Societies*, edited by Davide Nadali, 21–36. London: Bloomsbury Academic.

Corsi, Pietro. 2012. 'Idola Tribus: Lamarck, Politics and Religion in the Early Nineteenth Century'. In *The Theory of Evolution and Its Impact*, edited by Aldo Fasolo, 11–39. Milan: Springer Milan.

Cox, Rupert A. 2008. *The Culture of Copying in Japan: Critical and Historical Perspectives*. Japan Anthropology Workshop Series. London: Routledge.

Ćwiek, Andrzej. 2014. 'Old and Middle Kingdom Tradition in the Temple of Hatshepsut at Deir El-Bahari'. *Études et Travaux* 27: 61–93.

Czapkiewicz, Andrzej. 1968. 'Z historii badań nad toponomastyka Egiptu'. *Onomastica* 13: 345–52.

Daly, El Okasha. 2005. *Egyptology: The Missing Millennium. Ancient Egypt in Medieval Arabic Writings*. London: UCL Press.

Darnell, John C. 2014. 'The Stela of the Viceroy Usersatet (Boston MFA 25.632), His Shrine at Qasr Ibrim, and the Festival of Nubian Tribute under Amenhotep II'. *Égypte Nilotique et Méditerranéenne* 7: 239–76.

Davies, Norman de Garis. 1901. *The Rock Tombs of Sheikh Saïd.* Archaeological Survey of Egypt 10. London: Egypt Exploration Fund.

1905. *The Rock Tombs of el Amarna III: The Tombs of Huya and Ahmes.* Archaeological Survey of Egypt 15. London: Egypt Exploration Fund.

1943. *The Tomb of Rekh-mi-Rē' at Thebes.* Publications of the Metropolitan Museum of Art Egyptian Expedition 11. New York: Plantin Press.

Davies, Vanessa, and Dimitri Laboury. 2020. *The Oxford Handbook of Egyptian Epigraphy and Palaeography.* New York: Oxford University Press.

Deicher, Susanne. 2015. 'Einführung'. In *Die Liste: Ordnungen von Dingen Und Menschen in Ägypten,* edited by Susanne Deicher and Erik Maroko, 7–28. Berlin: Kadmos.

Deicher, Susanne, and Erik Maroko. 2015. *Die Liste: Ordnungen von Dingen und Menschen in Ägypten.* Berlin: Kadmos.

Den Doncker, Alexis. 2017. 'Identifying Copies in the Private Theban Necropolis: Tradition As Reception under the Influence of Self-Fashioning Processes'. In *(Re)Productive Traditions in Ancient Egypt: Proceedings of the Conference Held at the University of Liège, 6th–8th February 2013,* edited by Todd Gillen, 333–70. Liege: Presses universitaires de Liège.

Derrida, Jacques. 1978. *Writing and Difference,* translated by Alan Bass. Chicago, IL: University of Chicago Press.

Doležalová, Lucie. 2009. *The Charm of a List: From the Sumerians to Computerised Data Processing.* Newcastle upon Tyne: Cambridge Scholars.

Donadoni, Sergio. 1997. *The Egyptians.* Chicago, IL: University of Chicago Press.

Donker van Heel, Koenraad, and Ben Haring. 2003. *Writing in a Workmen's Village: Scribal Practice in Ramesside Deir El-Medina.* Egyptologische Uitgaven 16. Leiden: Nederlands Instituut voor het Nabije Oosten.

Dorn, Andreas. 2004. 'Die Lehre Amunnachts'. *Zeitschrift für ägyptische Sprache Und Altertumskunde* 131: 38–55.

Dorn, Andreas, and Stéphane Polis. 2016. 'Nouveaux Textes Littéraires Du Scribe Amennakhte (et Autres Ostraca Relatifs Au Scribe de La Tombe)'. *Bulletin de l'Institut Français d'Archéologie Orientale* 116: 57–96.

Dunham, Dows. 1938. 'The Biographical Inscriptions of Nekhebu in Boston and Cairo'. *Journal of Egyptian Archaeology* 24 (1): 1–8.

Eco, Umberto. 1989 (1962). *The Open Work,* translated by Annapaola Cancogni and David Robey. Cambridge, MA: Harvard University Press.

1995. *The Search for the Perfect Language: Making of Europe.* Oxford: Blackwell.

2009. *The Infinity of Lists.* New York: Rizzoli.

Edwards, Elizabeth. 2012. *The Camera As Historian: Amateur Photographers and Historical Imagination, 1885–1918*. Objects/Histories. Durham, NC: Duke University Press.

2015. 'Anthropology and Photography: A Long History of Knowledge and Affect'. *Photographies* 8 (3): 235–52.

Enmarch, Roland. 2008. *A World Upturned: Commentary on and Analysis of The Dialogue of Ipuwer and the Lord of All*. British Academy Postdoctoral Fellowship Monograph. Oxford: Published for The British Academy by Oxford University Press.

Erman, Adolf. 1927. *The Literature of the Ancient Egyptians: Poems, Narratives, and Manuals of Instruction from the Third and Second Millennia BC*, translated by Aylward M. Blackman. London: Methuen.

Eschenbrenner-Diemer, Gersande. 2017. 'From the Workshop to the Grave: The Case of Wooden Funerary Models'. In *Company of Images: Modelling the Imaginary World of Middle Kingdom Egypt (2000–15000 BC). Proceedings of the International Conference of the EPOCHS Project Held 18th–20th September 2014 at UCL, London*, edited by Stephen Quirke, Gianluca Miniaci, and Marilina Betrò, 133–91. Leuven: Peeters.

Eyre, Christopher. 2013. *The Use of Documents in Pharaonic Egypt*. Oxford Studies in Ancient Documents. Oxford: Oxford University Press.

Ezzamel, Mahmoud. 1997. 'Accounting, Control and Accountability: Preliminary Evidence from Ancient Egypt'. *Critical Perspectives on Accounting* 8 (6): 563–601.

2012. *Accounting and Order*. Routledge Studies in Accounting. London: Taylor and Francis.

Fasolo, Aldo (ed.). 2012. *The Theory of Evolution and Its Impact*. Milan: Springer Milan.

Faulkner, Raymond O. 1962. *A Concise Dictionary of Middle Egyptian*. Oxford: Griffith Institute.

Fischer-Elfert, Hans-Werner. 1986. *Die Satirische Streitschrift des Papyrus Anastasi I: Übersetzung und Kommentar*. Vol. 44. Ägyptologische Abhandlungen. Wiesbaden: Harrassowitz.

2017. 'Cross-Genre Correspondences: Wisdom, Medical, Mathematical and Oneirological Compositions from the Middle Kingdom to the Late New Kingdom'. In *(Re)Productive Traditions in Ancient Egypt: Proceedings of the Conference Held at the University of Liège, 6th–8th February 2013*, edited by Todd Gillen, 149–61. Liege: Presses universitaires de Liège.

2021. *Grundzüge einer Geschichte des Hieratischen*, Einführungen und Quellentexte zur Ägyptologie 14. Munster: Lit.

Fitzenreiter, Martin. 1995. 'Totenverehrung und soziale Repräsentation im thebanischen Beamtengrab der 18. Dynastie'. *Studien zur altägyptischen Kultur* 22: 95–130.

Frood, Elizabeth. 2007. *Biographical Texts from Ramessid Egypt*. Writings from the Ancient World 26. Atlanta, GA: Society of Biblical Literature.

2010. 'Social Structure and Daily Life: Pharaonic'. In *A Companion to Ancient Egypt*, vol. 1, edited by Alan B. Lloyd, 469–90. Chichester: Wiley-Blackwell.

Galán, José M., and Lucía Díaz-Iglesias Llanos 2020. 'The Overseer of the Treasury Djehuty in TT 11, Speos Artemidos, and Deir el-Bahari'. In *Text-Bild-Objekte im archäologischen Kontext: Festschrift für Susanne Bickel* edited by Kathrin Gabler, Rita Gautschy, Lukas Bohnenkämper et al., 151–69. Hamburg: Widmaier.

Gange, David. 2013. *Dialogues with the Dead: Egyptology in British Culture and Religion, 1822–1922*. Oxford: Oxford University Press.

Gardiner, Alan H. 1916. *Notes on the Story of Sinuhe*. Paris: Librairie Honoré Champion.

1937. *Late-Egyptian Miscellanies*. Bibliotheca Aegyptiaca 7. Brussels: Fondation égyptologique Reine Élisabeth.

1947. *Ancient Egyptian Onomastica*. Oxford: Oxford University Press.

1948. *Ramesside Administrative Documents*. London: Published on behalf of the Griffith Institute, Ashmolean Museum, Oxford by Oxford University Press.

Geoga, Margaret. 2021. 'New Insights into Papyrus Millingen and the Reception History of The Teaching of Amenemhat'. *Journal of Egyptian Archaeology* 107 (1–2): 225–38. https://doi.org/10.1177/03075133211050658.

Gertzen, Thomas L. 2017. *Nathaniel Julius Reich: Arbeit im Turm zu Babel*. 1. Auflage. Jüdische Miniaturen (Hentrich and Hentrich); Bd. 197. Berlin: Hentrich and Hentrich.

2020. 'Some Remarks on the "De-colonization" of Egyptology'. *Göttinger Miszellen* 261: 189–203.

Gestermann, Louise. 2005. *Die Überlieferung ausgewählter Texte altägyptischer Totenliteratur ('Sargtexte') in spätzeitlichen Grabanlagen*. Ägyptologische Abhandlungen 68. Wiesbaden: Harrassowitz.

Gillen, Todd J. 2014. 'Ramesside Registers of Égyptien de Tradition: The Medinet Habu Inscriptions'. In *On Forms and Functions: Studies in Ancient Egyptian Grammar*, edited by Jean Winand, Stéphane Polis, Eitan Grossman, and Andréas Stauder, 41–86. Hamburg: Widmaier.

2017. *(Re)Productive Traditions in Ancient Egypt: Proceedings of the Conference Held at the University of Liège, 6th–8th February 2013.* Aegyptiaca Leodiensia 10. Liege: Presses universitaires de Liège.

Glanville, Stephen Ranulph Kingdon. 1932. 'Scribes' Palettes in the British Museum: Part I'. *Journal of Egyptian Archaeology* 18 (1/2): 53–61.

Gnirs, Andrea M. 1996. 'Die Ägyptische Autobiographie'. In *Ancient Egyptian Literature: History and Forms*, edited by Antonio Loprieno, 191–241. Leiden: Brill.

Goedicke, Hans. 1967. *Königliche Dokumente aus dem alten Reich.* Ägyptologische Abhandlungen 14. Wiesbaden: Harrassowitz.

1977. *The Protocol of Neferyt (The Prophecy of Neferti).* Johns Hopkins Near Eastern Studies. Baltimore, MD: Johns Hopkins University Press.

Goelet Jr, Ogden. 2008. 'Writing Ramesside Hieratic: What the Late Egyptian Miscellanies Tell Us about Scribal Education'. In *Servant of Mut: Studies in Honor of Richard A. Fazzini*, edited by Sue H. D'Auria, 102–10. Leiden: Brill.

2010. 'Observations on Copying and the Hieroglyphic Tradition in the Production of the Book of the Dead'. In *Offerings to the Discerning Eye: An Egyptological Medley in Honor of Jack A. Josephson*, edited by Sue H. D'Auria, 121–32. Leiden: Brill.

2015. 'Verse Points, Division Markers, and Copying'. *Bulletin of the Egyptological Seminar* 19: 347–58.

Goldwasser, Orly. 2002. *Prophets, Lovers and Giraffes: Wor(l)d Classification in Ancient Egypt.* Classification and Categorization in Ancient Egypt 3; Göttinger Orientforschungen, 4. Reihe: Ägypten 38. Wiesbaden: Harrassowitz.

Goldwasser, Orly, and Colette Grinevald. 2012. 'What Are "Determinatives" Good For?' In *Lexical Semantics in Ancient Egyptian*, edited by Eitan Grossman, Stéphane Polis, and Jean Winand, 17–53. Hamburg: Widmaier.

Goody, Jack. 1977. *The Domestication of the Savage Mind.* Themes in the Social Sciences. Cambridge: Cambridge University Press.

Goody, Jack, and Ian Watt. 1963. 'The Consequences of Literacy'. *Comparative Studies in Society and History* 5 (3): 304–45.

Graefe, Erhart, and Matthieu Heerma van Voss. 1993. 'Papyrus Leiden T3 Oder: Über das Kopieren von Texten durch Altägyptische Schreiber'. *Oudheidkundige Mededelingen Uit Het Rijksmuseum van Oudheden* 73: 23–8.

Grandet, Pierre. 1994. *Le Papyrus Harris I (BM 9999)*. Bibliothèque d'étude 109. Cairo: Institut Français d'Archéologie Orientale.

——— 2018. 'The "Chapter on Hierarchy" in Amenope's Onomasticon (# 67–125)'. In *The Ramesside Period in Egypt: Studies into Cultural and Historical Processes of the 19th and 20th Dynasties*, edited by Sabine Kubisch and Ute Rummel, 127–37. Berlin: De Gruyter.

Griffin, Carrie, and Emer Purcell. 2018. *Text, Transmission, and Transformation in the European Middle Ages, 1000–1500*. Cursor Mundi (Turnhout, Belgium), vol. 34. Turnhout: Brepols.

Griffith, Francis Llewellyn 1897. *Egyptian Literature*. New York: J. A. Hill and Company.

Griffith, Francis Llewellyn, and Kate Bradbury Griffith. 1917. 'Egyptian Literature. Critical Introduction'. In *The Library of the World's Best Literature: An Anthology in Thirty Volumes*. New York: Warner Library Company.

Griffith, Francis Llewellyn, and Flinders Petrie. 1889. *Two Hieroglyphic Papyri from Tanis*. London: Trübner and Company.

Grimal, Nicolas. 2006. 'Les Listes de Peuples Dans l'Égypte Du Deuxième Millénaire Av. J.-C. et La Géopolitique Du Proche-Orient'. In *Timelines: Studies in Honour of Manfred Bietak*, vol. 1, edited by Ernst Czerny, Irmgard Hein, Angela Schwab, Dagmar Melman, and Hermann Hunger, 107–19. Leuven: Peeters en Departement Oosterse Studies.

Gunn, Battiscombe. 1906. *The Instruction of Ptah-Hotep and the Instruction of Ke'gemni: The Oldest Books in the World*. London: Murray.

Hafemann, Ingelore with contributions by Altägyptisches Wörterbuch, Anja Weber, 'pMMA 27.3.560' (Object ID J47XXWESOVF7DI52K5Z7SDNOQM) https://thesaurus-linguae-aegyptiae.de/object/J47XXWESOVF7DI52K5Z7SDNOQM. In *Thesaurus Linguae Aegyptiae*, Corpus issue 17, Web app version 2.01, 12/15/2022, edited by Tonio Sebastian Richter and Daniel A. Werning by order of the Berlin-Brandenburgische Akademie der Wissenschaften and Hans-Werner Fischer-Elfert and Peter Dils by order of the Sächsische Akademie der Wissenschaften zu Leipzig (accessed 30 April 2023).

Hagen, Fredrik. 2012. *An Ancient Egyptian Literary Text in Context: The Instruction of Ptahhotep*. Orientalia Lovaniensia Analecta 218. Leuven: Peeters en Departement Oosterse Studies.

——— 2013. 'Constructing Textual Identity: Framing and Self-Reference in Egyptian Texts'. In *Ancient Egyptian Literature: Theory and Practice*, edited by Roland Enmarch and Verena M. Lepper, 185–209. Oxford: Oxford University Press.

2019a. 'Libraries in Ancient Egypt, c.1600–800 BCE'. In *Libraries before Alexandria: Ancient Near Eastern Traditions*, edited by Kim Ryholt and Gojko Barjamovic, 244–318. Oxford: Oxford University Press.

2019b. 'New Copies of Old Classics: Early Manuscripts of Khakheperreseneb and The Instruction of a Man for His Son'. *Journal of Egyptian Archaeology* 105 (2): 177–208.

Hagen, Fredrik, and Daniel Soliman. 2018. 'Archives in Ancient Egypt, 2500–1000 BCE'. In *Manuscripts and Archives: Comparative Views on Record-Keeping*, edited by Michael Friedrich, Alessandro Bausi, Christian Brockmann, and Sabine Kienitz, 71–170. Berlin: De Gruyter.

Hannig, Rainer. 2003. *Ägyptisches Wörterbuch I. Altes Reich und Erste Zwischenzeit*. Mainz: Philipp von Zabern.

Haring, Ben J. J. 2015. 'Hieratic Drafts for Hieroglyphic Texts?' In *Ägyptologische 'Binsen'-Weisheiten I–II: Neue Forschungen und Methoden der Hieratistik. Akten Zweier Tagungen in Mainz im April 2011 und März 2013*, edited by Ursula Verhoeven, 67–84. Stuttgart: Franz Steiner.

2020. 'The Survival of Pharaonic Ostraca: Coincidence or Meaningful Patterns?' In *Using Ostraca in the Ancient World: New Discoveries and Methodologies*, vol. 32, edited by Clementina Caputo and Julia Lougovaya, 89–108. Berlin: De Gruyter.

Harnad, Stevan. 2005. 'To Cognize Is to Categorize: Cognition Is Categorization'. *Handbook of Categorization in Cognitive Science*, January: 19–43.

Harpur, Yvonne 1987. *Decoration in Egyptian Tombs of the Old Kingdom: Studies in Orientation and Scene Content*. Studies in Egyptology. London: Routledge and Kegan Paul.

Harpur, Yvonne, and Paolo Scremin. 2006. *The Chapel of Kagemni: Scene Details*. Egypt in Miniature 1. Reading: Oxford Expedition to Egypt.

2010. *The Chapel of Niankhkhnum & Khnumhotep: Scene Details*. Egypt in Miniature 3. Reading: Oxford Expedition to Egypt.

Hartwig, Melinda K. 2004. *Tomb Painting and Identity in Ancient Thebes, 1419–1372 BCE*. Monumenta Aegyptiaca 10. Brussels: Fondation égyptologique Reine Élisabeth.

Hassan, Khaled. 2016. 'An 18th Dynasty Wooden Board in the Egyptian Museum of Cairo, JE 95750 – CG 25366'. *Egyptian Journal of Archaeological and Restoration Studies* 6 (2): 125–32.

2016. 'Some 18th Dynasty Hieratic Ostraca from Deir El-Bahri'. *Bulletin de l'Institut Français d'Archéologie Orientale* 115: 179–229.

2017. 'An 18th Dynasty Writing-Board from Saqqara in the Cairo Museum (Prophety of Neferti – CGC 25224, JE 32972)'. *Bulletin de l'Institut Français d'Archéologie Orientale* 117: 261.

Hassan, Selim. 1943. *Excavations at Gîza IV: 1932–1933.* Cairo: Government Press, Bulaq.

Hayes, William C. 1957. 'Varia from the Time of Hatshepsut'. *Mitteilungen des Deutschen Archäologischen Instituts, Abteilung Kairo* 15: 78–90.

Hodder, Ian. 2012. *Entangled: An Archaeology of the Relationships between Humans and Things.* Malden, MA: Wiley-Blackwell.

Hoey, Michael. 2005. *Lexical Priming: A New Theory of Words and Language.* Abingdon: Routledge.

Hofmann, Eva. 1995. *Das Grab des Neferrenpet gen. Kenro (TT 178).* Theben 9. Mainz: Zabern. Nach Vorarbeiten von Machmud Abd el-Raziq, mit Beiträgen von Karl-J. Seyfried.

Hornung, Erik. 2001. *The Secret Lore of Egypt: Its Impact on the West.* Ithaca, NY: Cornell University Press.

Iversen, Erik. 1961. *The Myth of Egypt and Its Hieroglyphs in European Tradition.* Copenhagen: G. E. C. Gad.

Jakeman, Jane. 2005. 'Sketched Symbols (*Egyptology: The Missing Millennium: Ancient Egypt in Medieval Arabic Writings*)(Book Review)'. *Times Literary Supplement* 5353: 8.

Janssen, Jac. J. 1987. 'On Style in Egyptian Handwriting'. *Journal of Egyptian Archaeology* 73, 161–7.

1992. 'Literacy and Letters at Deir El-Medîna'. In *Village Voices: Proceedings of the Symposium 'Texts from Deir El-Medîna and Their Interpretation', Leiden, May 31–June 1, 1991*, edited by Robert Johannes Demarée and Arno Egberts, 81–94. Leiden: Centre of Non-Western Studies, Leiden University.

Jéquier, Gustave. 1938. *Le monument funéraire de Pepi II. vol. II.* Fouilles à Saqqarah. Cairo: Imprimérie de l'Institut français d'archéologie orientale.

Jirásková, Lucie. 2020. 'The Reception of Ancient Egypt and Its Script in Renaissance Europe'. In *The Oxford Handbook of Egyptian Epigraphy and Palaeography*, edited by Dimitri Laboury and Vanessa Davies, 193–204. New York: Oxford University Press.

Jones, Dilwyn. 2000. *An Index of Ancient Egyptian Titles, Epithets and Phrases of the Old Kingdom.* BAR International Series 866 (1–2). Oxford: Archaeopress.

Kahl, Jochem. 1999. *Siut - Theben.* Leiden: Brill.

Kahl, Jochem, and Martin von Falck. 2000. 'Die Rolle von Saqqara und Abusir bei der Überlieferung altägyptischer Jenseitsbücher'. In *Abusir and*

Saqqara in the Year 2000, edited by Miroslav Bárta and Jaromír Krejčí, 215–28. Prague: Academy of Sciences of the Czech Republic, Oriental Institute.

Kanawati, Naguib. 2011. 'Art and Gridlines: The Copying of Old Kingdom Scenes in Later Periods'. In *Abusir and Saqqara in the Year 2010*, vol. 2, edited by Miroslav Bárta, Filip Coppens, and Jaromír Krejčí, 483–96. Prague: Czech Institute of Egyptology, Faculty of Arts, Charles University in Prague.

Kanawati, Naguib, and Mahmud Abder-Raziq. 1999. *The Teti Cemetery at Saqqara. Volume V: The Tomb of Hesi*. Australian Centre for Egyptology: Reports 13. Warminster: Aris and Phillips.

Kanawati, Naguib, and Ali Hassan. 1997. *The Teti Cemetery at Saqqara. Volume II: The Tomb of Ankhmahor*. Australian Centre for Egyptology: Reports 9. Warminster: Aris and Phillips.

Kanawati, Naguib, and Alexandra Woods. 2009. *Artists of the Old Kingdom: Techniques and Achievements*. [Cairo]: Supreme Council of Antiquities.

Kanawati, Naguib, Alexandra Woods, Sameh Shafik, and Effy Alexakis. 2010. *Mereruka and His Family, Part III.1: The Tomb of Mereruka*. Australian Centre for Egyptology: Reports 29. Oxford: Aris and Phillips.

Keller, Cathleen A. 1997. 'Private Votives in Royal Cemeteries: The Case of KV 9'. *Varia Aegyptiaca* 10 (2–3): 139–15.

Kessler, Dieter. 1990. 'Zur Bedeutung der Szenen des täglichen Lebens in den Privatgräbern (II): Schreiber und Schreiberstatue in den Gräbern des AR'. *Zeitschrift für ägyptische Sprache Und Altertumskunde* 117: 21–43.

Klotz, David, and Andréas Stauder. 2020. *Enigmatic Writing in the Egyptian New Kingdom I: Revealing, Transforming, and Display in Egyptian Hieroglyphs*. Zeitschrift für ägyptische Sprache Und Altertumskunde – Beihefte 12. Berlin: De Gruyter.

Krutzsch, Myriam. 2008. 'Falttechniken an altägyptischen Handschriften'. In *Ägypten lesbar machen – die klassische Konservierung/Restaurierung von Papyri und neuere Verfahren: Beiträge des 1. Internationalen Workshops der Papyrusrestauratoren, Leipzig 7.–9. September 2006*, edited by Jörg Graf and Myriam Krutzsch, 71–83. Berlin: De Gruyter.

2014. 'Materialtechnische Beobachtungen während der Restaurierung'. In *Magika hieratika in Berlin, Hannover, Heidelberg und München*, edited by Hans-W. Fischer-Elfert, 1–74. Berlin: De Gruyter.

2016. 'Reading Papyrus As Writing Material'. *British Museum Studies in Ancient Egypt and Sudan* 23: 57–69.

Laboury, Dimitri. 2012. 'Tracking Ancient Egyptian Artists, a Problem of Methodology: The Case of the Painters of Private Tombs in the Theban

Necropolis during the Eighteenth Dynasty'. In *Art and Society: Ancient and Modern Contexts of Egyptian Art: Proceedings of the International Conference Held at the Museum of Fine Arts, Budapest, 13–15 May 2010*, edited by Katalin Anna Kóthay, 199–208. Budapest: Museum of Fine Arts.

2016. 'Le scribe et le peintre: À propos d'un scribe qui ne voulait être pris pour un peintre'. In *Aere perennius: mélanges égyptologiques en l'honneur de Pascal Vernus*, edited by Philippe Collombert, Dominique Lefèvre, Stéphane Polis, and Jean Winand, 371–96. Leuven: Peeters.

2017. 'Tradition and Creativity: Toward a Study of Intericonicity in Ancient Egyptian Art'. In *(Re)Productive Traditions in Ancient Egypt: Proceedings of the Conference Held at the University of Liège, 6th–8th February 2013*, edited by Todd Gillen, 229–58. Liege: Presses universitaires de Liège.

2022a. 'Artistes et écriture hiéroglyphique dans l'Égypte des pharaons'. *Bulletin de la Société Française d'Égyptologie* 207: 37–67.

2022b. 'Le signe comme image... '. In *Guide des écritures de l'Égypte ancienne*, edited by Stéphane Polis, 144–9. Cairo: Institut français d'archéologie orientale.

2022c. '... ou l'image comme signe'. In *Guide des écritures de l'Égypte ancienne*, edited by Stéphane Polis, 150–3. Cairo: Institut français d'archéologie orientale.

Laboury, Dimitri, and Alisée Devillers. 2022. 'The Ancient Egyptian Artist: A Non-existing Category?' In *Ancient Egyptian Society: Challenging Assumptions, Exploring Approaches*, edited by Danielle Candelora, Nadia Ben-Marzouk, and Kara Cooney. Abingdon: Routledge.

Lacau, Pierre, and Henri Chevrier. 1977. *Une chapelle d'Hatshepsout à Karnak I*. Cairo: IFAO.

Landgráfová, Renata. 2015. '"Creative Copying": Notes on Text Tradition and Alteration Evidenced in Multiple-Occuring Texts in the Shaft Tomb of Iufaa at Abusir'. In *Text: Wissen - Wirkung - Wahrnehmung: Beiträge des Vierten Münchner Arbeitskreises Junge Ägyptologie (MAJA 4), 29.11. Bis 1.12.2013*, edited by Burkhard Backes, Alexandra Verbovsek, Gregor Neunert et al., 31–58. Wiesbaden: Harrassowitz.

Latour, Bruno. 2005. *Reassembling the Social: An Introduction to Actor-Network-Theory*. Clarendon Lectures in Management Studies. Oxford: Oxford University Press.

LD = Lepsius, C. R. 1849–59. *Denkmaeler aus Aegypten und Aethiopien*, Nach den Zeichnungen der von Seiner Majestät dem Koenige von Preussen, Friedrich Wilhelm IV., nach diesen Ländern gesendeten und in den Jahren

1842–1845 ausgeführten wissenschaftlichen Expedition. Berlin: Nicolaische Buchhandlung.

Leitz, Christian. 2014. *Die Gaumonographien in Edfu und ihre Papyrusvarianten: Ein überregionaler Kanon kultischen Wissens im spätzeitlichen Ägypten: Soubassementstudien III.* Studien zur spätägyptischen Religion 9. Wiesbaden: Harrassowitz.

Lesko, Leonard H. 1994. 'Literature, Literacy, and Literati'. In *Pharaoh's Workers: The Villagers of Deir El Medina*, edited by Leonard H. Lesko, 131–44, 185–8. Ithaca, NY: Cornell University Press.

Lichtheim, Miriam. 1988. *Ancient Egyptian Autobiographies Chiefly of the Middle Kingdom: A Study and an Anthology.* Orbis Biblicus et Orientalis 84. Freiburg: Universitätsverlag.

Lincke, Eliese-Sophia, and Frank Kammerzell. 2012. 'Egyptian Classifiers at the Interface of Lexical Semantics and Pragmatics'. In *Lexical Semantics in Ancient Egyptian*, edited by Eitan Grossman, Stéphane Polis, and Jean Winand, 55–112. Hamburg: Widmaier.

Lloyd, Alan B. 2010. *A Companion to Ancient Egypt.* Blackwell Companions to the Ancient World. Chichester: Wiley-Blackwell.

Loprieno, Antonio. 1996. 'Defining Egyptian Literature: Ancient Texts and Modern Literary Theory'. In *The Study of the Ancient Near East in the Twenty-First Century: The William Foxwell Albright Centennial Conference*, edited by Jerrold S. Cooper and Glenn M. Schwartz, 209–32. Winona Lake, IN: Eisenbrauns.

2001. *La pensée et l'écriture: pour une analyse sémiotique de la culture égyptienne: Quatre séminaires à l'école pratique des hautes études, section des sciences religieuses, 15–27 mai 2000.* Paris: Cybele.

Luft, Ulrich, Margarete Büsing, and Marianna Szücs. 2006. *Urkunden zur Chronologie der Späten 12. Dynastie: Briefe aus Illahun.* Österreichische Akademie der Wissenschaften, Denkschriften der Gesamtakademie 34. Wien: Verl. der Österr. Akad. der Wiss.

Lüscher, Barbara. 2015. 'Kursivhieroglyphische Ostraka als Textvorlagen: Der (Glücks-)Fall TT 87'. In *Ägyptologische 'Binsen'-Weisheiten I–II: Neue forschungen und Methoden der Hieratistik. Akten zweier Tagungen in Mainz im April 2011 Und März 2013*, edited by Ursula Verhoeven, 85–117. Stuttgart: Franz Steiner.

Lydon, Jane, Elizabeth Edwards, Jennifer Tucker, and Patricia Hayes. 2016. *Photography, Humanitarianism, Empire.* London: Taylor and Francis Group.

MacKenzie, John M. 1995. *Orientalism: History, Theory and the Arts.* Manchester: Manchester University Press.

Malek, Jaromir. 2000. 'Old Kingdom Rulers As "Local Saints" in the Memphite Area during the Middle Kingdom'. In *Abusir and Saqqara in the Year 2000*, edited by Miroslav Bárta and Jaromír Krejčí, 241–58. Prague: Academy of Sciences of the Czech Republic, Oriental Institute.

Manuelian, Peter der. 1993. *Living in the Past: Studies in Archaism of the Egyptian Twenty-Sixth Dynasty*. Studies in Egyptology. London: Kegan Paul International.

Manuelian, Peter der. 1996. 'Presenting the Scroll: Papyrus Documents in Tomb Scenes of the Old Kingdom'. In *Studies in Honor of William Kelly Simpson*, vol. 2, edited by Peter der Manuelian, 561–88. Boston, MA: Department of Ancient Egyptian, Nubian and Near Eastern Art, Museum of Fine Arts.

2003. *Slab Stelae of the Giza Necropolis*. Publications of the Pennsylvania–Yale Expedition to Egypt 7. New Haven, CT: Peabody Museum of Natural History of Yale University.

Martin, Geoffrey T. 1979. *The Tomb of Ḥetepka and Other Reliefs and Inscriptions from the Sacred Animal Necropolis, North Saqqâra, 1964–1973*. London: Egypt Exploration Society.

1989. *The Memphite Tomb of Ḥoremḥeb Commander-in-Chief of Tutʿankhamūn: I, The Reliefs, Inscriptions, and Commentary*. Excavation Memoir. London: Egypt Exploration Society.

Maspero, Gaston. 1895. *Histoire ancienne des peuples de l'Orient classique*. Paris: Hachette.

Massart, Adhémar. 1959. 'À Propos des "Listes" dans les textes Égyptiens funéraires et magiques'. In *Studia Biblica et Orientalia, Edita a Pontificio Instituto Biblico Ad Celebrandum Annum L Ex Quo Conditum Est Institutum, Volumen III: Oriens Antiquus*, 227–46. Rome: Pontificio Istituto biblico.

Mathieu, Bernard. 2013. 'Grammaire et politique: réflexions sur quelques empreintes idéologiques dans la terminologie linguistique des grammaires de l'égyptien ancien'. In *Ägyptologen und Ägyptologien zwischen Kaiserreich und Gründung der beiden Deutschen Staaten: Reflexionen zur Geschichte und Episteme eines Altertumswissenschaftlichen Fachs im 150. Jahr der Zeitschrift für Ägyptische Sprache und Altertumskunde*, edited by Susanne Bickel, Hans-Werner Fischer-Elfert, Antonio Loprieno, Sebastian Richter, and Lutz Popko, 437–56. Berlin: Akademie Verlag Berlin.

McDowell, Andrea. 1996. 'Student Exercises from Deir El-Medina: The Dates'. In *Studies in Honor of William Kelly Simpson*, vol. 2, edited by

Peter der Manuelian, 601–8. Boston, MA: Department of Ancient Egyptian, Nubian and Near Eastern Art, Museum of Fine Arts.

Meeks, Dimitri. 1980–2. *Année lexicographique, tome 1–3* (1977–9).

Morales, Antonio J. 2017. *The Transmission of the Pyramid Texts of Nut: Analysis of Their Distribution and Role in the Old and Middle Kingdoms*. Studien zur Altägyptischen Kultur, Beihefte 19. Hamburg: Helmut Buske.

Morenz, Ludwig D. 2022. 'Hieroglyphische Hermeneutik: ein dreifacher Kulturkontakt im Byzantinischen 12. Jh. n. Chr'. *Zeitschrift für ägyptische Sprache Und Altertumskunde* 149 (1): 72–9.

Olsen, Rune R. 2018. 'Socioeconomic Aspects of Ancient Egyptian Private Tomb Construction: A Study on New Kingdom Tomb Volumetrics As Economic Markers', unpublished PhD thesis, University of Copenhagen.

Osing, Jürgen. 1997. 'School and Literature in the Ramesside Period'. In *L'impero Ramesside: Convegno Internazionale in onore di Sergio Donadoni*, edited by Isabella Brancolli, Emanuele M. Ciampini, Alessandro Roccati, and Loredana Sist, 131–42. Rome: Università degli Studi di Roma.

Osterhammel, Jürgen. 2015. *The Transformation of the World: A Global History of the Nineteenth Century*. America in the World. Princeton, NJ: Princeton University Press.

Parkinson, Richard B. 1996a. 'Individual and Society in Middle Kingdom Literature'. In *Ancient Egyptian Literature: History and Forms*, edited by Antonio Loprieno, 137–55. Leiden: Brill.

1996b. 'Types of Literature in the Middle Kingdom'. In *Ancient Egyptian Literature: History and Forms*, edited by Antonio Loprieno, 298–312. Leiden: Brill.

1996c. 'Khakheperreseneb and Traditional Belles Lettres'. In *Studies in Honor of William Kelly Simpson* 2, edited by Peter der Manuelian, 647–54. Boston, MA: Department of Ancient Egyptian, Nubian and Near Eastern Art, Museum of Fine Arts.

1997. *The Tale of Sinuhe and Other Ancient Egyptian Poems, 1940–1640 BC*. Oxford: Clarendon.

2002. *Poetry and Culture in Middle Kingdom Egypt: A Dark Side to Perfection*. Athlone Publications in Egyptology and Ancient Near Eastern Studies. London: Continuum.

2009. *Reading Ancient Egyptian Poetry: Among Other Histories*. Chichester: Wiley-Blackwell.

2012. *The Tale of the Eloquent Peasant: A Reader's Commentary*. Lingua Aegyptia, Studia Monographica 10. Hamburg: Widmaier.

Parkinson, Richard, and Stephen Quirke. 1995. *Papyrus*. Egyptian Bookshelf. London: British Museum Press.

Parkinson, Richard, and Neal Spencer. 2017. 'The Teaching of Amenemhat I at Amara West: Egyptian Literacy Culture in Upper Nubia'. In *Nubia in the New Kingdom: Lived Experience, Pharaonic Control and Indigenous Traditions*, edited by Neal Spencer, Michaela Binder, and Anna Stevens, 213–23. Leuven: Peeters.

Patch, Diana Craig. 2005. 'The Shrines to Hathor at Deir el-Bahri'. In *Hatshepsut: From Queen to Pharaoh*, edited by Catharine H. Roehrig, Renée Dreyfus, and Cathleen A. Keller, 173. New York: Metropolitan Museum of Art.

Peet, T. Eric. 1931. *A Comparative Study of the Literatures of Egypt, Palestine, and Mesopotamia: Egypt's Contribution to the Literature of the Ancient World. Schweich Lectures 1929*. London: Published for the British Academy by HMilford, Oxford University Press.

Pinarello, Massimiliano S. 2015. *An Archaeological Discussion of Writing Practice: Deconstruction of the Ancient Egyptian Scribe*. GHP Egyptology 23. London: Golden House.

Polis, S. (ed.). 2022. *Guide des écritures de l'Égypte antique*. Cairo: Institut Français d'Archéologie Orientale.

Popko, Lutz. 2014. 'History-Writing in Ancient Egypt'. *UCLA Encyclopedia of Egyptology* 1 (1). https://escholarship.org/uc/item/73v96940#author.

Posener, Georges. 1950. 'Section Finale d'une Sagesse Inconnue (Recherches Littéraires, II)'. *Revue d'égyptologie* 7: 71–84.

Posener-Kriéger, Paule. 1991. 'Aspects économiques des nouveaux papyrus d'Abousir'. In *Akten des vierten internationalen Ägyptologen Kongresses München 1985. Band 4: Geschichte, Verwaltungs- und Wirtschaftsgeschichte, Rechtsgeschichte, Nachbarkulturen*, edited by Sylvia Schoske, 167–76. Hamburg: Buske.

Posener-Kriéger, Paule, Miroslav Verner, and Hana Vymazalová. 2006. *Abusir X: The Pyramid Complex of Raneferef. The Papyrus Archive*. Excavations of the Czech Institute of Egyptology. Prague: Czech Institute of Egyptology, Charles University.

Power, Arthur. 2001 (1974). *Conversations with James Joyce*. Dublin: Dalkey Archive Press.

Ptaḥ-hetep, and Battiscombe George Gunn. 1906. *The Instruction of Ptah-Hotep and the Instruction of Ke'gemni: The Oldest Books in the World*, translated with an introduction by Battiscombe George Gunn. Wisdom of the East. London: Murray.

Quack, Joachim F. 2008. 'Geographie als Struktur in Literatur und Religion'. In *Altägyptische Weltsichten: Akten des Symposiums zur historischen Topographie und Toponymie Altägyptens vom 12.–14.Mai in München*, edited by Arnulf Schlüter, Katrin Schlüter, and Faried Adrom, 131–57. Wiesbaden: Harrassowitz.

2011. 'Textedition, Texterschließung, Textinterpretation'. In *Methodik und Didaktik in der Ägyptologie: Herausforderungen eines kulturwissenschaftlichen Paradigmenwechsels in den Altertumswissenschaften*, edited by Burkhard Backes, Alexandra Verbovsek, and Catherine Jones, 533–49. Munich: Wilhelm Fink.

2015. 'Ägyptische Listen und ihre Expansion in Unterricht und Repräsentation'. In *Die Liste: Ordnungen von Dingen und Menschen in Ägypten*, edited by Susanne Deicher and Erik Maroko, 51–86. Berlin: Kadmos.

2020a. 'Eine spätzeitliche Handschrift der Lehre des Cheti (Papyrus Berlin P 14423)'. In *Ein Kundiger, der in die Gottesworte Eingedrungen ist: Festschrift für den Ägyptologen Karl Jansen-Winkeln Zum 65. Geburtstag*, edited by Jan Moje, Vincent Pierre-Michel Laisney, and Shih-Wei Hsu, 233–51. Munster: Zaphon.

2020b. 'Zwei Fragmente religiöser Geographie'. In *The Carlsberg Papyri 15: Hieratic Texts from Tebtunis. Including a Survey of Illustrated Papyri*, edited by Andrea Kucharek, Joachim F. Quack, Kim Ryholt et al., 135–40. Copenhagen: Museum Tusculanum Press.

Quirke, Stephen. 1996. 'Archive'. In *Ancient Egyptian Literature: History and Forms*, edited by Antonio Loprieno, 379–401. Leiden: Brill.

2004a. *Egyptian Literature 1800 BC: Questions and Readings*. Egyptology (Golden House) 2. London: Golden House.

2004b. *Titles and Bureaux of Egypt, 1850–1700 BC*. Egyptology (Golden House) 1. London: Golden House.

2009. 'Contexts for the Lahun Lists'. In *Verba Manent: Recueil d'études Dédiées à Dimitri Meeks Par Ses Collègues et Amis*, vol. 2, edited by Frédéric Servajean and Isabelle Régen, 363–86. Montpellier: Université Paul Valéry.

Ragazzoli, Chloé C. D. 2013. 'The Social Creation of a Scribal Place: The Visitors' Inscriptions in the Tomb Attributed to Antefiqer (TT 60) (with Newly Recorded Graffiti)'. *Studien Zur Altägyptischen Kultur* 42: 269–323.

2016. 'Toponymie et Listes: Un Onomasticon Fragmentaire de Basse Époque (P.BnF Ms. Égyptien 245, 1–2)'. In *Décrire, Imaginer, Construire l'espace: Toponymie Égyptienne de l'Antiquité Au Moyen Âge*, edited by

Claire Somaglino and Sylvain Dhennin, 69–91. Cairo: Institut français d'archéologie orientale.

2017a. 'Beyond Authors and Copyists: The Role of Variation in Ancient Egyptian and New Kingdom Literary Production'. In *(Re)Productive Traditions in Ancient Egypt: Proceedings of the Conference Held at the University of Liège, 6th–8th February 2013*, edited by Todd Gillen, 95–126. Liege: Presses universitaires de Liège.

2017b. 'Présence divine et obscurité de la tombe au Nouvel Empire: À propos des graffiti des Tombes TT 139 et TT 112 à Thèbes (Avec Édition et Commentaire)'. *Bulletin de l'Institut Français d'Archéologie Orientale* 117: 357–407.

2019. *Scribes: les artisans du texte en Égypte ancienne*, preface by Christian Jacob. Paris: Belles Lettres.

Ragazzoli, Chloé, Ömür Harmanşah, Chiara Salvador, and Elizabeth Frood (eds.). 2018. *Scribbling through History: Graffiti, Places and People from Antiquity to Modernity.* London: Bloomsbury Academic.

Redford, Donald B. 1986. *Pharaonic King-Lists, Annals and Day-Books: A Contribution to the Study of the Egyptian Sense of History.* SSEA Publications 4. Mississauga: Benben.

Regulski, Ilona. 2010. *A Palaeographic Study of Early Writing in Egypt.* Orientalia Lovaniensia Analecta 195. Leuven: Peeters en Departement Oosterse Studies.

Ritner, Robert K. 1993. *The Mechanics of Ancient Egyptian Magical Practice.* Studies in Ancient Oriental Civilization 54. Chicago, IL: Oriental Institute of the University of Chicago.

Robins, Gay. 1991. 'Composition and the Artist's Squared Grid'. *Journal of the American Research Center in Egypt* 28: 41–54.

2001. 'The Use of the Squared Grid As a Technical Aid for Artists in Eighteenth Dynasty Painted Theban Tombs'. In *Colour and Painting in Ancient Egypt*, edited by W. Vivian Davies, 60–2. London: British Museum Press.

Roehrig, Catharine H. 2005. 'Painting in the Early Eighteenth Dynasty'. In *Hatshepsut: From Queen to Pharaoh*, edited by Catharine H. Roehrig, Renée Dreyfus, and Cathleen A. Keller, 44–5. New York: Metropolitan Museum of Art.

Ryholt, Kim, and Gojko Barjamovic. 2019. *Libraries before Alexandria: Ancient Near Eastern Traditions.* Oxford: Oxford University Press.

Ryholt, Kim, Andrea Kucharek, Joachim F. Quack et al. 2020. *The Carlsberg Papyri 15: Hieratic Texts from Tebtunis. Including a Survey of Illustrated Papyri*. CNI Publications 45. Copenhagen: Museum Tusculanum Press.

Scalf, Foy. 2016. 'From the Beginning to the End: How to Generate and Transmit Funerary Texts in Ancient Egypt'. *Journal of Ancient Near Eastern Religions* 15 (2): 202–23.

Shirley, J. J. 2010. 'Viceroys, Viziers & the Amun Precinct: The Power of Heredity and Strategic Marriage in the Early 18th Dynasty'. *Journal of Egyptian History* 3 (1): 73–113.

Simon, Henrike. 2013. *'Textaufgaben': Kulturwissenschaftliche Konzepte in Anwendung auf die Literatur der Ramessidenzeit*. Hamburg: Helmut Buske.

Spalinger, Anthony J. 2002. *The Transformation of an Ancient Egyptian Narrative: P.Sallier III and the Battle of Kadesh*. Göttinger Orientforschungen, 4. Reihe: Ägypten 40. Wiesbaden: Harrassowitz.

——— 2003. 'New Kingdom Eulogies of Power: A Preliminary Analysis'. In *Es werde niedergelegt als Schriftstück: Festschrift für Hartwig Altenmüller zum 65. Geburtstag*, edited by Nicole Kloth, Karl Martin, and Eva Pardey, 415–28. Hamburg: Buske.

Staring, Nico. 2019. 'From Landscape Biography to the Social Dimension of Burial: A View from Memphis, Egypt, c. 1539–1078 BCE.' In *Perspectives on Lived Religion: Practices – Transmission – Landscape*, edited by Nico Staring, Lara Weiss, and Huw Twiston Davies, 207–23. Leiden: Sidestone.

Stauder, Andréas. 2013a. 'L'émulation du passé à l'ère thoutmoside: La dimension linguistique'. In *Vergangenheit und Zukunft: Studien zum historischen Bewusstsein in der Thutmosidenzeit*, edited by Susanne Bickel, 77–125. Basel: Schwabe.

——— 2013b. *Linguistic Dating of Middle Egyptian Literary Texts: Dating Egyptian Literary texts, Göttingen, 9–12 June 2010, 2*. Lingua Aegyptia, Studia Monographica 12. Hamburg: Widmaier.

——— 2018. 'Staging Restricted Knowledge: The Sculptor Irtysen's Self-Presentation (ca. 2000 BC)'. In *The Arts of Making in Ancient Egypt: Voices, Images, and Objects of Material Producers 2000–1550 BC*, edited by Gianluca Miniaci, Juan Carlos Moreno García, Stephen Quirke, and Andréas Stauder, 239–71. Leiden: Sidestone.

——— 2020. 'Scripts'. In *The Oxford Handbook of Egyptology*, edited by Elizabeth Bloxam and Ian Shaw, 869–96. Oxford: Oxford University Press.

Stauder-Porchet, Julie. 2021a. 'Werre: A Royal Inscription of the Early Fifth Dynasty'. *Studien zur Altägyptischen Kultur* 50: 309–27.

2021b. 'L'inscription lapidaire de la parole royale chez les particuliers à la Ve dynastie'. In *Questionner le sphinx: Mélanges offerts à Christiane Zivie-Coche*, vol. 1, edited by Ivan Guermeur, Christophe Thiers, Laurent Coulon, Philippe Collombert, 137–64. Bibliothèque d'étude 178. Cairo: Institut Français d'Archéologie Orientale.

Stauder-Porchet, Julie, Elizabeth Frood, and Andréas Stauder. 2020. *Ancient Egyptian Biographies: Contexts, Forms, Functions*. Wilbour Studies in Egyptology and Assyriology 6. Atlanta, GA: Lockwood.

Strudwick, Nigel. 1985. *The Administration of Egypt in the Old Kingdom: The Highest Titles and Their Holders*. London: KPI.

Sundermeyer, Annette. 2020. 'Interpretations and Reuse of Ancient Egyptian Hieroglyphs in the Arabic Period (Tenth–Sixteenth Centuries CE)'. In *The Oxford Handbook of Egyptian Epigraphy and Palaeography*, edited by Dimitri Laboury and Vanessa Davies, 176–92. New York: Oxford University Press.

Taylor, John H. 2010. *Spells for Eternity: The Ancient Egyptian Book of the Dead*. London: British Museum.

Töpfer, Susanne, Paolo Del Vesco, and Federico Poole (eds.). 2022. *Deir el-Medina: Through the kaleidoscope. Proceedings of the International Workshop, Turin 8th–10th October 2018*. Museo Egizio: Formazione e ricerca. Torino: Museo Egizio; Franco Cosimo Panini.

Traunecker, Claude. 2014. 'The "Funeral Palace" of Padiamenope: Tomb, Place of Pilgrimage, and Library. Current Research'. In *Thebes in the First Millennium BC*, edited by Julia Budka, Elena Pischikova, and Kenneth Griffin, 205–34. Newcastle upon Tyne: Cambridge Scholars Publishing.

Urk I = Kurt Sethe, *Urkunden des Alten Reichs*. Urkunden des aegyptischen Altertums, I. Leipzig: J. C. Hinrichs, 1903–84.

Urk IV = Kurt Sethe, H.Wolfgang Helck et al. *Urkunden der 18. Dynastie*. Urkunden des aegyptischen Altertums, IV. Leipzig: J. C. Hinrichs, 1903–84.

Vandier, J. 1964. *Manuel d'archéologie Égyptienne, Tome IV: Bas-Reliefs et Peintures – Scènes de La Vie Quotidienne*. Paris: Éditions A. et J. Picard et Cie.

Velde, Herman te. 1986. 'Scribes and Literacy in Ancient Egypt'. In *Festschrift J. H. Hospers: Scripta Signa Vocis. Studies about Scripts, Scriptures, Scribes and Languages in the Near East*, edited by H. L. J. Vanstiphout, 253–64. Groningen:

Verhoeven, Ursula, 2020. *Dipinti von Besuchern des Grabes N13.1 in Assiut*. The Asyut Project. Wiesbaden: Harrassowitz.

Vernus, Pascal. 1995. *Essai sur la conscience de l'histoire dans l'égypte pharaonique*. Bibliothèque de l'École des hautes études. IVe section, Sciences historiques et philologiques 332. Paris: HChampion.

——— 2013. 'The Royal Command (wD-nsw): A Basic Deed of Executive Power'. In *Ancient Egyptian Administration*, edited by Juan Carlos Moreno García, 259–340. Leiden: Brill.

——— 2022. 'Script and Figurativity: Modelling the Relationship between Image and Writing in Ancient Egypt'. In *Wege zur frühen Schrift: Niltal und Zweistromland*, edited by Ludwig D. Morenz, Andréas Stauder, and Beryl Büma, 335–421. Berlin: EB-Verlag Dr. Brandt.

Vymazalová, Hana. 2015. 'The Administration and Economy of the Pyramid Complexes and Royal Funerary Cults in the Old Kingdom', unpublished PhD thesis, Charles University in Prague.

Walle, Baudouin van de. 1963. 'Problèmes Relatifs Aux Méthodes d'enseignement Dans l'Égypte Ancienne.' In *Les Sagesses Du Proche-Orient Ancien: Colloque de Strasbourg 17–19 Mai 1962*, 191–207. Paris: Presses Universitaires de France.

Wb = Adolf Erman and Hermann Grapow. 1926–31. *Wörterbuch der ägyptische Sprache*. Berlin: Akademie.

Webb, David. 2012. *Foucault's Archaeology: Science and Transformation*. Edinburgh: Edinburgh University Press.

Weeks, Kent R. 1979. 'Art, Word, and the Egyptian World View'. In *Egyptology and the Social Sciences: Five Studies*, edited by Kent R. Weeks, 59–81. Cairo: American University in Cairo Press.

Wengrow, David. 2020. 'Egyptology and Cognate Disciplines', in *The Oxford Handbook of Egyptology*, edited by Ian Shaw and Elizabeth Bloxam, 48–64. Oxford: Oxford University Press.

Westerfeld, Jennifer T. 2019. *Egyptian Hieroglyphs in the Late Antique Imagination*. Philadelphia: University of Pennsylvania Press.

White, Hayden. 1986. 'Historical Pluralism', *Critical Inquiry* 12 (3): 480–93.

Wilkinson, John G. 1878. *The Manners and Customs of the Ancient Egyptians*. New ed. Revised and corrected by Samuel Birch. London: J. Murray.

Winand, Jean. 2022. 'Athanasius Kircher et Le Déchiffrement Des Hiéroglyphes: Réalité Ou Fiction?' *Revue de l'histoire Des Religions* 239 (2): 217–55.

Winlock, Herbert E. 1923. 'The Egyptian Expedition 1922–1923: The Museum's Excavations at Thebes'. *Bulletin of the Metropolitan Museum of Art* 18 (12.2): 11–39.

——— 1955. *Models of Daily Life in Ancient Egypt, from the Tomb of Meket-Rē' at Thebes*. Metropolitan Museum of Art (New York). Egyptian Expedition.

Publications of the Metropolitan Museum of Art Egyptian Expedition 18. Cambridge, MA: Published for the Metropolitan Museum of Art by Harvard University Press.

Wittgenstein, Ludwig. 1953 (2009). *Philosophische Untersuchungen = Philosophical Investigations*. 4th ed. Revised by Peter M. S. Hacker and Joachim Schulte. Chichester: Wiley-Blackwell.

Wyrick, Jean. 2016. *Steps to Writing Well with Additional Readings*. 10th ed. Fort Collins: Colorado State University.

Yates, Frances A. 2014. *The Art of Memory*. London: The Bodley Head.

Ziegler, Christiane. 1990. *Catalogue des stèles, peintures et reliefs égyptiens de l'Ancien Empire et de la Première Période Intermédiaire: vers 2686–2040 avant J.-C.* Paris: Éditions de la Réunion des musées nationaux.

1993 *Le mastaba d'Akhethetep: Une chapelle funéraire de l'Ancien Empire*. Paris: Éditions de la Réunion des musées nationaux.

Zivie, Alain. 2013. *La tombe de Thoutmes, directeur des peintres dans la Place de Maât (BUB. I.19)*. Les tombes du Bubasteion à Saqqara 2. Toulouse: Caracara.

Acknowledgements

This Element could not have been written without the support, encouragement, and patience of numerous colleagues and friends within and outside our institutions. We are especially thankful to Gianluca Miniaci, Juan Carlos Moreno Garcìa, and Anna Stevens for the invitation to write this Element, as well as their support for this project, which was written during the lockdowns surrounding COVID-19 and its aftermath. We would like to thank the two anonymous reviewers for their helpful and insightful comments.

Orly Goldwasser and Daniel Gonzalez León generously discussed drafts of a few sections, while conversations with Julia Hamilton, Lucía Díaz-Iglesias Llanos, Margaret Geoga, Aurore Motte, and Ian Rutherford benefitted many parts of the Element. To them and many others, we are truly grateful.

Cambridge Elements ≡

Ancient Egypt in Context

Gianluca Miniaci
University of Pisa

Gianluca Miniaci is Associate Professor in Egyptology at the University of Pisa, Honorary Researcher at the Institute of Archaeology, UCL – London, and Chercheur associé at the École Pratique des Hautes Études, Paris. He is currently co-director of the archaeological mission at Zawyet Sultan (Menya, Egypt). His main research interest focuses on the social history and the dynamics of material culture in Middle Bronze Age Egypt and its interconnections between the Levant, Aegean, and Nubia.

Juan Carlos Moreno García
CNRS, Paris

Juan Carlos Moreno García (PhD in Egyptology, 1995) is a CNRS senior researcher at the University of Paris IV–Sorbonne, as well as lecturer on social and economic history of ancient Egypt at the École des Hautes Études en Sciences Sociales (EHESS) in Paris. He has published extensively on the administration, socio-economic history, and landscape organization of ancient Egypt, usually in a comparative perspective with other civilizations of the ancient world, and has organized several conferences on these topics.

Anna Stevens
University of Cambridge and Monash University

Anna Stevens is a research archaeologist with a particular interest in how material culture and urban space can shed light on the lives of the non-elite in ancient Egypt. She is Senior Research Associate at the McDonald Institute for Archaeological Research and Assistant Director of the Amarna Project (both University of Cambridge).

About the Series

The aim of this Elements series is to offer authoritative but accessible overviews of foundational and emerging topics in the study of ancient Egypt, along with comparative analyses, translated into a language comprehensible to non-specialists. Its authors will take a step back and connect ancient Egypt to the world around, bringing ancient Egypt to the attention of the broader humanities community and leading Egyptology in new directions.

Cambridge Elements $\equiv$

Ancient Egypt in Context

Elements in the Series

Printed in the USA
CPSIA information can be obtained
at www.ICGtesting.com
CBHW071928030924
13955CB00010B/1000